# A Rebel's Road Home

*sequel to "A Northern Rebel"*

# A Rebel's Road Home

*sequel to "A Northern Rebel"*

By

John J. Schaffer

This book is dedicated to God; for giving me the inspiration and the talent to complete another book; to my wife for her undying love, help and public relations work on my behalf; and to all my loyal fans and readers for their love and gratitude of my first novel This novel is also dedicated to those who requested a sequel thereby bringing the characters to life and affording them a continued existence while caring about what happens to them. I feel truly blessed.

*"There is no greater agony than bearing an untold story inside you."*
*"History, despite its wrenching pain, cannot be unlived, but if faced with courage, need not be lived again."*
-Maya Angelou,
Poet, Novelist, Actress, Educator, Civil Rights Activist,
1928 – 2014


*"If your actions inspire others to dream more, learn more, do more and become more, you are a leader."*
-John Quincy Adams,
American President, 1767-1848


*"Cowardice asks: Is it safe? Expediency asks: Is it politic? Vanity asks: Is it popular? But conscience asks: Is it right?"*
- William Morley Punshon,
English clergy man, 1824 -1881


*"When the power of love overcomes the love of power, the world will know peace."*
- Jimi Hendrix,
Musician, 1942-1970


*"You receive the reward you earn on earth."*
- John J Schaffer
Author, Musician

# Chapters

# Chapter 1

## Shadows of the Past

It was the ninth of April, 1865 and the news of the end of the Civil War rippled across the New England town of Boston and straight into the Hartford residence where a celebration was ensuing. Jameson, Delilah, his wife, their child, Dawnalee, Nanny, their adopted grandmother and all the other individuals Jameson had managed to free from his plantation in South Carolina were commemorating the victory and what it meant for all present…the end of enslavement. Jameson had procured a few bottles of champagne and as the corks popped, the sparkling wine was poured and enjoyed by all the guests toasting freedom and justice for all their people.

A man was standing outside, across the street, draped in a dark coat, barely visible under the flickering lamplight. He was intently watching the house waiting until he was sure all the guests were present and enough liquor had been consumed, then he carefully made his way across the cobblestone road.

The party had barely begun with everyone so elated that no one saw the figure of a man approaching the front door. His wide brimmed hat was pulled low over his face to hide his identity and his hideous plan.

Jameson Hartford was a tall blue eyed gentleman whose dirty blonde hair was showing signs of age with wisps of grey covering each temple.

It made him look all the more distinguished. Delilah was a beautiful woman of color whose warm complexion, light brown eyes and pixie haircut made her look much younger than her years; and effectively hid her painful past. Dawnalee was the cutest 4 year old, a perfect mixture of color and love, while Nanny never seemed to change and still looked like the quintessential grandmother, a little too heavy with her hair covered by a wrapped scarf.

The celebration was gaining momentum as the shadowy figure crept around the side of the residence and peered in the window. He identified everyone's location and the general layout of the room. He placed his hand into his pocket and felt the pistol which he grasped firmly in his hand. He climbed the porch steps and positioned his hand on the doorknob. It did not turn, it must be locked. He reached for the chain and tugged on it causing the bell attached to jingle.

As Millie, the house servant unlocked the door and opened it; the figure pushed his way in, waving his gun, slamming the door behind him. He looked directly at his victim and screamed, "Justice has finally found you Jameson Hartford and the verdict is death!"

The small crowd gasped, shrieked and ran for cover.

Jameson stood there in front of the figure and calmly said, "Who are you and what do you want with me?"

"Don't you recognize your own nephew, uncle?" the figure said as he took off the hat, revealing a badly burned but still recognizable face. "Are you surprised? I did not die in that fire at the mansion. I ran back into it to save my wife. Remember you left her in there to die. She didn't perish, I saved her."

"Jebediah, Jeb, I'm so glad you are alive, and Madeline is she alright?

"She is fine. We both managed to jump out the back window. She broke her leg in the fall but it has since healed. I wish I could say the same for my injuries. Look uncle, my face my arm, half my body burnt. It took me months to heal; and all that time all I could think about was you and what you did to me. When I was able, I rebuilt my Serenity mansion, where I hoped to live happily ever after with my wife, but that was not to be."

He took a deep breath and continued, "The confederate army found me and had me arrested for desertion. They put me back on the front lines, hoping I would die, but I did not. I killed a lot of Yankees and thought of you each time I pulled the trigger. Now, after all this time, I am here for my retribution.

"Jeb I am so sorry for what happened, but I did not leave Madeline in that house."

"Yes you did, uncle and now you will pay for what happened to me."

"Jeb, I didn't want anyone to be hurt, that was you and the other townsfolk who wouldn't let me free my workers and wanted to silence me. You all came to my home to kill me and to re-enslave the people I just freed. Those trespassers started the fire. She was stuck upstairs; we were all trying to get out alive."

"Enough of your lies! When I realized the war was lost and the end was near I again deserted the army so I could come here and find you, just to pay you back. I see you're still with that colored wife of yours. I would have thought you would have come to your senses by now and thrown her aside."

"We're married, Jeb, and we love each other. We have a child."

"Well isn't that nice, then she will make a good looking widow," Jeb said as he raised the pistol and pointed it at Jameson.

"No, please, he's telling you the truth, begged Delilah, "I loved Madeline, and I would never have left her to die in the fire."

"I don't care what you say, I know the truth. Say goodbye to your husband."

"No," Delilah screamed as she ran forward.

Jameson grabbed her and held her out of harm's way as he again tried to reason with the irrational Jebediah.

"Jeb, think about what you going to do, you won't get away with it. You will be arrested and spend the rest of your life in jail, or maybe even hung. What about Madeline? Don't you want to be with her?"

Jebediah pondered the idea and momentarily hesitated from carrying out his heinous task.

The front door was suddenly and unexpectedly thrown open and in walked Martha Barrington, the Hartford's neighbor. She was carrying a sheet cake which she had made to celebrate the occasion. Jeb was stunned and briefly looked away from his prey. That was the opening Jameson needed to lunge forward and engage Jeb in a hand to hand battle for the small firearm. In the excitement, Martha dropped the cake to the floor. As the two men wrestled back and forth, Jeb inadvertently stepped onto the fallen cake, losing his footing. He fell backward with Jameson right on top of him. The gun discharged with a loud bang, and the bullet found a different, innocent victim… Martha Barrington.

It was not a life threatening wound, but she was bleeding badly. Nanny and Delilah went to her aid attempting to stop the flow of blood. Jebediah was temporarily knocked unconscious enabling Jameson to disarm him and render him incapacitated. A few of the guests ran to get the police. Jameson and his friends held him until the law arrived.

Jebediah was arrested but even as he was dragged off to jail, he swore, "You should have killed me when you had the chance, uncle, I will return and have my revenge. No jail cell can keep me from killing you. You will never have a moment's peace, I promise you."

Jameson wondered if Jebediah wasn't right; perhaps he should have ended this part of his life while he had the chance; but he never possessed such hatred that would have allowed him to enact such a deed. He would have to wait for the final act to play out and hoped he survived.

Martha was examined by the doctor and after a few stitches she was returned to her home where she was told to get plenty of rest. The party was tabled for a later date and all the guests returned to their homes.


In the days that followed, Delilah would spend a good deal of time attending to Martha and trying to nurse her back to health. In spite of it all, Martha always wanted to look her best, as was her style; face made up, hair perfectly coiffed and, as always, impeccably dressed.

Delilah had suffered through a bad pregnancy and a hard delivery on the road from South Carolina to freedom in Boston and was having a difficult time conceiving a second child. She had had two miscarriages and was reluctant to try again not wanting to suffer the unbearable sadness again. She even avoided Jameson; much to his chagrin. She was more than happy to spend her time attending to Martha Barrington, after all they were best friends and she owed her so much. Delilah thought of her as her mother, since she was told her real mother, whom she was forcibly taken from when she was young, had died on some unknown plantation in South Carolina.

Martha was healing nicely from the wound, when she contracted a form of influenza, which being a new disease to the area and had no known cure. Because of her age and weakened condition it became a serious ailment. She suffered fits of high fever and deliria, tempered with periods of improved health. One night, because she seemed to be in remission, Delilah was getting ready to return to her own home.

"I'll be back first thing in the morning, Martha, you have a restful night."

Martha begged her, "Please dear, open the window so when it is time, my guardian angel would not be barred from coming for my soul and we can both easily pass through this world into the next."

Delilah told her, "I don't want you to speak such nonsense. You are going to get better, you hear me? I don't want to hear any talk of death either. It is cold outside and the besides the night air is not good for you."

Martha called Delilah over, pulled a string of pearls from her jewelry box and pressed them into Delilah's hand.

"These are for you, my dear. They were a gift from my late husband. They are very expensive pearls. They glow in the moonlight like there are bits of fire trapped inside each one of the beads."

"I can't accept this, Martha my dear. They are yours and you should keep them."

"Nonsense Delilah, I want you to have them. Go to the window and see how they shimmer in the moonlight."

Delilah walked over to the window and held them out into the darkness. When the moonlight hit them, each bead glowed like a small distinct star. It was beautiful.

"I really can't accept these Martha."

"Yes you can and I will not take no for an answer. Now, return to your home and your husband, I'm so tired, I need to sleep."

Delilah thanked her for the pearls, kissed Martha's head, wished her a good night and returned to her own home.

Later that evening as Delilah showed Jameson the beautiful pearls and how they glowed in the moonlight; he placed them around her neck and gently snapped the clasp. She would never again remove them.

He kissed her and told her how beautiful she looked. She returned the kiss as they lie on the bed about to join together in love.

"Let me close that window, it's chilly outside tonight."

Delilah was suddenly reminded of Martha's request to leave the window open and she felt compelled to look out her own window at the Barrington home. It was an overcast night and she could scarcely see anything, until the moon emerged from behind one of the clouds. There she could plainly see Martha's window … open. She called to Jameson and they quickly donned their robes and raced over to Martha's residence.

Delilah unlocked the door and they sprinted up the stairs to the bedroom. There on her bed was Martha Barrington. There was a smile on her face, but she was not breathing. Delilah checked her pulse, there was none. She looked at Jameson and they both stared at the open window; strangely the curtains were blowing outward and then abruptly the breeze shifted and the frosty night air blew into the room, giving them both a chill. Delilah began to weep and fell into Jameson's arms.

The doctor was called and Martha Barrington was officially pronounced dead. Delilah and Jameson mourned for a great friend and a great lady who had helped them through many difficult situations. She would never be forgotten. Her life was celebrated at a service before the good Lord and all her friends and afterward she was laid to rest in her family crypt alongside her husband who had died many years earlier.

The next afternoon, Delilah, Jameson and Nanny were sitting at the kitchen table reminiscing about the wonderful lady and all she did to help them, especially through some trying times. She helped Jameson start his own banking business after he was fired from his former job for being married to Delilah. She taught Delilah everything she needed to know to become a real lady and leave her indentured servant life behind her once and for all. She helped them plan their wedding and stood godmother for Dawnalee. She was a true friend who only noticed the good in people and did not judge them on their race, creed, or color.

The sound of the doorbell interrupted their recollections. This time it was an attorney charged with settling the estate of Martha Barrington. To everyone's surprise, Martha left everything; all her worldly possessions and all her money to Delilah. Martha was one of the richest women in Boston; this now made Delilah one of the wealthiest women in Boston and, no doubt, the richest black woman in the United States of America!

As Delilah signed the papers designating her as the sole heir, she queried, "Why would she leave it all to me, James?"

"You were her best friend and she loved you."

"What could I possibly do with so much money?"

"You'll think of something, sweetheart."

"James, you are the banker. Do I invest it? Do I spend it? I want to put it to good use…"

Delilah's eyes grew larger and her face suddenly lit up as an idea crossed her mind.

"What is it darling?  You look like the fox that got caught in the hen house."

"I just thought of something. I'll tell you later after I've worked out all the details."

"You're going to put the money in my bank, aren't you darling?"

"Just be patient my dear husband and all will be revealed."

She sported a mischievous smile as she calmly strode away. Nanny, Jameson and the lawyer just stared at each other.

"I seen looks like that before and it always spelled trouble," said Nanny.

Martha Barrington's estate included her house, all her furnishings, jewelry and substantial cash holdings.  Delilah had the job of liquidating all the assets but could not bring herself to sell anything. Instead, she decided to give the property to Nanny who, as a slave, was never allowed to own anything. Nanny, overcome with happiness, cried for a full day, sobbing and thanking Delilah and praising the Lord.

Satisfied with her decisions so far, Delilah decided it was time to put her initial plan into action. She contacted Martha's lawyer, Mr. Wells, and told him to meet her the following morning at the First United Bank of Boston. Delilah arrived ahead of him, looking absolutely gorgeous in her green dress with matching bonnet and shoes. The bank was a foreboding building of red brick with only one door for entry and exit ably guarded by an armed security man. It seemed impenetrable to all except a determined young black woman. Delilah calmly and assuredly entered the bank but was quickly stopped dead in her tracks by the doorman.

"Can I help you, uh miss?"

"I want to see the president of the bank, Mr. Porter."

All the patrons of the bank stopped whatever they were doing, and an eerie silence fell over the normally noisy structure. Altogether, they stared at the beautiful black woman, wondering what she wanted in their bank.

"What may I ask is the nature of your business? We don't usually contract with people of your, uh stature."

"You best take me to Mr. Porter now or you'll be looking for a new job tomorrow."

The doorman was about to argue further when Mr. Wells came in and told him to announce them immediately. He politely obeyed and ushered them in to the president's office.

Mr. Porter was clad in his finest navy blue suit, his thinning grey locks were neatly combed back to disguise the obvious lack of hair, and his spectacles were worn low on his nose as he gazed out menacingly over the rims. He looked even more intimidating sitting behind his huge oak desk. He wanted to know why a "colored" woman was sitting in his office and addressed his question directly to Mr. Wells purposely ignoring Delilah.

The undaunted black woman immediately opened her mouth and said, "I wish to make a deposit in your bank."

Mr. Porter imagining that a black woman had limited funds, if any, again ignored her and spoke to Mr. Wells, "What amount are we speaking of, sir?"

Delilah was getting angrier and angrier at being treated like a second class citizen and spoke right out, "I… wish to make a deposit, a very large deposit."

When she announced the amount, Mr. Porter's mouth dropped open and he again placed his foot directly into it yet again.

"How did you come by such a large amount of money?" this time speaking directly to Delilah.

"I inherited it and if you are not interested, I know of several other banks that would be glad to take my money."

He was astonished at the amount thinking how it would almost double his worth and eagerly accepted it, changing his whole demeanor toward Delilah and now treating her with the utmost respect, gushing all over her, complementing her on her appearance and offering her a drink.

The necessary papers were drawn up, signed and the two visitors departed with Mr. Porter continuing to fawn all over Delilah, even kissing her hand. The doorman even bid her a good day as she left.

Outside, Mr. Wells wished Delilah much success in her endeavor and went on his way. Delilah felt empowered and marveled at the difference money could make in her life. She would no longer be treated as a second class citizen; she was rich and important especially to those people who didn't care about her before. A devilish smirk filled her face as she felt her plan coming to fruition.

Jameson and Nanny wondered what she had done with the money and kept pressuring her with countless questions to which she calmly replied, "Just wait, you'll see when I think it is time."

They just gazed at each other with puzzled looks and shrugged their shoulders. What else could they do?

Delilah bided her time, dodging all inquiries until she felt the time was right, giggling under her breath at her carefully staged plot.

A few weeks later, Delilah returned to the bank, waiting just out of sight for Mr. Porter to exit for his usual liquor lunch afternoon respite. She easily gained admittance, no one dared to stop her, in fact; they pretended they were glad to see her. She proceeded to one of the bank executives and demanded all her money be returned to her at once, as she heard that this particular bank was not solvent and was in danger of collapse.

"I heard Mr. Porter approved some bad loans and will lose a fortune on them, causing this bank to fail and have to close its doors forever."

She insisted all her funds be transferred immediately to Jameson's bank, a reputable institution. She spoke loud enough to be sure she was heard by all the other investors.

The teller in the cage behind the counter tried to ensure her that whatever gossip she heard was totally incorrect and the bank was completely solid. Any efforts to quiet her by bank personnel were ignored; Delilah just spoke all the more loudly and insisted the she receive all her funds immediately.

"If you are indeed solvent, then why won't you give me my money, or don't you have it? Is it already lost? I demand it at once!"

The teller, manager and associates were beginning to panic and quickly complied with the lady's demand in the hopes that she would quiet down and just leave. But, the damage was done and the news spread rapidly. The repercussions were astounding and a run on the bank began as depositor after depositor also demanded all their money at once. Assurances by bank personnel fell on deaf ears as the assets in the vault grew smaller and smaller eventually emptying all cash and bonds forcing the bank to prematurely close. This unprecedented occurrence caused the once powerful institution to run out of currency and completely collapse. Public trust was gone and the bank was unable to reopen.

The act ruined Mr. Porter, who just happened to be the father of Prudence, a woman who was instrumental in destroying Jameson's previous career. Luckily, Jameson was subsequently saved by Martha Barrington, who helped him start his own bank. Prudence was now as penniless as she had left Jameson those few years ago. Revenge was indeed sweet, Delilah thought to herself.

When Jameson found out, he was upset, "You shouldn't have done that, Lilah."

"I knew you would not like what I was going to do, so I didn't tell you. She deserved it, James, as did all the rest of them."

"Yes she did deserve it, but the whole plan makes me a little worried. Lilah, money changes people. Please don't change; I love you just the way you are."

"I will never change my feelings toward you, James, but now that I have money, no one will ever treat me with disrespect again. People will stand up and take notice of me. A rich woman of African descent, a former slave; they will have to accept me and deal with me. Money makes me important."

"You were always important to me, Lilah and you always will be. Don't become the kind of person you hated."

Delilah just giggled and walked away, but there was a cockiness to her walk.

The next morning, April 16, 1865 the Hartford residence was stunned once again, this time by the sound of the town crier in the street, "President Lincoln was assassinated last night at Ford's Theater. I repeat Abraham Lincoln is dead from an assassin's bullet. It occurred last night in Washington. Read all about it in today's Boston News."

Jameson reached into his pocket and produced a copper cent which he gave to Dawnalee and told her to run outside and get a copy of the newspaper. The child eagerly grabbed the coin and sprinted out of the house returning in a matter of a minute with today's paper. Jameson produced another copper cent and pressed it into Dawnalee's little hand, telling her to go and feed her piggy bank, which the child enthusiastically did, running up the stairs to her bedroom as Nanny shouted, "Slow down child, before you fall and hurt yourself."

Jameson, Delilah, and Nanny couldn't believe this unexpected turn of events. What would become of the world now? Would slavery be reinstated? Would a new war be inevitable? Again they were sitting at the kitchen table wondering what it all meant and hoping the newspaper was somehow wrong. Delilah was staring off into the distance when suddenly she had another inspiration.

"I know what we should do James. We have to go back to South Carolina and help my people. They are now legally free, but they have no skills. They were forbidden to learn how to read and write or to go to school. I can help them. I can start schools, teach them. Open businesses and give them jobs, pay them a salary and give them lives, reasons to live. Oh James, this will put Martha's money to such good use. Isn't it a great idea?"

"Lilah, what you want to do is noble and I support you 100%, but it will be dangerous there. We don't know what to expect, especially with the death of the president. If you thought we were hated before, just wait until now. I don't think we should do it. We have a family to think of."

"What about my people and their families. They deserve a chance at a decent life, don't they? And I can give them that chance. Please James, it's important to me."

She then thought of the perfect argument that would change Jameson's mind: "Besides you can finally fulfill your dream and run the plantation with hired workers and prove to all of them that your idea would have worked if they had only given you the chance you always wanted."

Jameson just smiled. He knew what she wanted to do was moral and right, but he feared for their safety. He could continue to argue but he knew from the look on her face and the tone of her voice that she would persevere until he changed his mind. There was something different about her, a change in demeanor and appearance. He could not put his finger on it and besides, he could not say no to her, so he simply nodded, *yes*.

"When do you want to leave?"

"Immediately."

"Should we leave Dawnalee here with Nanny?" Jameson inquired.

Nanny shook her head and said, "If y'all are going to go, you ain't leavin' me here, I'm going with you. Somebody got to look out for us Hartford's. Besides, who's gonna cook for you and mend your clothes and…"

"Yes, you should come, Nanny, along with Dawnalee," Delilah agreed, "It will be good for her to see where she came from. We should all go together and face whatever happens as a family."

Jameson was reluctant but knew it meant a lot to Delilah and besides he did want to see his family plantation again, the one Jebediah supposedly rebuilt.

The next days were spent in preparation. They packed their belongings and purchased their train tickets. Jameson brought two pistols and two rifles along with ample ammunition, just to be safe. He left his bank in the capable hands of his vice president and the workers he had so diligently trained. They took some cash and coins with them but the bulk of Delilah's money would be wired as needed to the Willow Hills bank, hoping it was still there. They bid farewell to their friends and vowed they would eventually come back. The plans were set in motion for a return to Serenity.

Prudence Porter was furious when she learned her father's bank had to close its doors. The bank had been in their family for generations, handed down from father to son since anyone could remember, and now it was all gone. At first she was shocked and appalled, but her initial reaction had long since worn off and now she wanted to find the cause and the responsible party. A little light detective work on her part revealed the culprit, one Delilah Hartford, and Prudence was hell bent on retribution.

She had visited this household once before in an attempt to blackmail Jameson. When he would not acquiesce to her wishes she had him fired from his job, leaving him and Delilah without any income. Now she returned with fire in her eyes to make both Delilah and Jameson pay for their actions.

Prudence marched right up to the front door and pounded on the huge wooden entryway. Millie opened the door and Prudence pushed her out of the way and barged right in, demanding to see either Hartford. Millie politely informed her that they were not at home.

"When will they be back?" Prudence inquired.

"I'm not sure miss; they went back down south to their other home."

"They did what?"

"Yes ma'am, would you care to leave a message?"

"No, that won't be necessary; I intend to deliver my message in person."

Prudence, frustrated, turned and strutted away, determined she would have her revenge, at any cost.

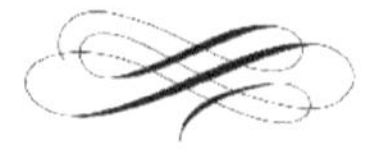

# Chapter 2

## *Ashes of the War*

The train ride to South Carolina was largely uneventful. The cars were not at full capacity as most people felt it was unsafe to travel. Yet, there they were going home to a place that was less than hospitable the last time they were there. In fact, they were hated and persecuted for Jameson's idea to free all his workers and replace them with hired employees, thereby decreeing that slavery was not necessary to successfully run a plantation and make it profitable. It was ironic that they were threatened and almost killed for trying to outlaw slavery, a belief that now was the law of the nation.

As the locomotive pulled into Maryland, the last stop north of the Mason/Dixon line, most passengers evacuated the train. The conductor asked them if they wanted to continue and if they knew the danger. Jameson reluctantly nodded and they proceeded into Dixie and on to South Carolina sleeping as much as their worried minds would allow before their trek southward.

Gazing out the windows, they could see the remnants of the war. There were burned out areas, sometimes as far as the eye could see. There were large holes in the ground no doubt caused by continued bombardments and battles. The area had suffered greatly in the war and there was no telling what they would find when they arrived at their destination. They prayed silently.

The train at last pulled into Charleston and as they embarked, they were shaken by all the destruction, charred buildings and scorched earth. There was debris everywhere and broken glass was strewn across the sidewalks and street. Large holes were visible where flying cannonballs finally met the earth. There was an ever increasing influx of young rebel soldiers dragging themselves home hoping to find the former life they remembered and fought so valiantly to protect. They hoped their residences were still intact; though most of them were not. These soldiers were maimed by a terrible war, most had lost limbs, were skinny as rails and bore horrific scars from the many battles they had fought. It was a sad sight. What did it mean for Jameson, Delilah, Nanny and Dawnalee; only time would tell.

They had forgotten how hot and musty the weather was, even in April. The four years in the cool New England climate left them ill prepared for the drastic change. They were dressed for cooler weather and had to remove layers of clothing to become as comfortable as possible. It would be a long journey to the plantation.

Jameson found a livery stable and managed to acquire a coach with two horses that could comfortably accommodate them and their luggage. He quickly loaded their belongings, helped the ladies on board and started the journey to what he hoped would be a safe refuge. The road was bumpy and occasionally strewn with dead decaying bodies, wearing both blue and grey uniforms. The unusually warm weather only contributed to the stench which filled the air. *What a waste of humanity*, he thought.

As they rumbled further down the road, a troop of soldiers, confederate soldiers, came riding up the road from the opposite direction. They rode rank and file, side by side, two by two, blocking up the entire thoroughfare and forcing Jameson to pull his coach off the main path and into the gully on the side of the road.

"Hey, watch where you're going," he shouted.

The captain of the troop did not even give him a passing glance but looked straight ahead and maintained a steady gallop. The rest of the men smirked as they passed and yelled at him, "Get off the road, and pay us the proper respect you Yankee trash."

Some soldiers swore and some cursed at the supposed northerners as they paraded two abreast, past the befuddled travelers. A few even spat at them trying to make a contest out of it and see which soldier could spit the farthest and smear the northerners with their spittle. Jameson supposed his and his passenger's attire gave them away and he would have to rectify that situation immediately upon reaching their destination.

"Don't they know the war is over?" Nanny screamed from inside the coach. "Those darn fools, don't they know they lost."

The soldiers vanished as quickly as they appeared but the coach was hopelessly stuck and Jameson could not get the wheels back on the gravel road. He needed Delilah to drive the horses as he had to push from behind to try and free the wheels from the muddy channel into which they were forced. With his back planted against the coach, he pushed and lifted with his legs and finally managed to hoist the wheels back onto the road, allowing them to continue on their journey.

They had barely traveled another mile when a little black girl ran crying out of the woods and reeds directly in front of the coach. The horses whinnied and reared up on their hind legs. Delilah succeeded in stopping them without hitting the little girl. She was clad in a torn dress and her little face and shoes were soiled. Her hair was braided in pigtails and she was visibly scared to death. Jameson jumped off the coach and approached the frightened child. She was terrified of him and began to cry and scream, "Don't hurt me, please, don't hurt me."

Delilah came running and cuddled the little child in her arms, telling her there was nothing to worry about and no one was going to hurt her. She calmed down and they pressed her as to where her mother and father were. She pointed off the road into the weeds and Jameson went to investigate.

He was stunned by what he spied. There lying in the gully, on the side of the road was the naked body of a young black woman left to die. She was covered from head to toe in black tar and feathers. He reached down and checked her pulse, there was no heartbeat; she was dead, but the body was still warm, indicating this atrocity had only just occurred maybe a few hours earlier.

"What is it James?"

"Stay there Lilah. Don't come over here. I don't want you to see this."

He ran to retrieve a blanket, swathed the body and carried it back to the coach. Delilah could not help but see what had occurred.

"James, who would do such a horrible thing to that poor woman?"

"I don't know but I sure hope we don't run into them. I pray we made the right decision in returning here."

Delilah was frightened but was determined to continue and complete her mission.

She turned to the little girl and said, "We will take care of you now honey. You'll be alright. What is your name sweetheart?"

"Ruby Rose."

"Well Ruby Rose, do you have any family around here?"

Ruby Rose shrugged her shoulders as if she did not know.

"That's ok baby, you can be our little girl now if you would like."

Ruby Rose shook her head yes and held onto Delilah with all her strength. Delilah looked to Jameson for approval and, of course, he also nodded yes.

The little girl was placed into the coach with Nanny and Dawnalee; Delilah continued to ride up front next to Jameson.

"You poor little thing, we'll take care of you, won't we Dawnalee?" Nanny said.

The rest of the trip was uneasy with Jameson and Delilah keeping a sharp lookout. Jameson held his gun close by, just in case.

Finally, they approached what used to be the road which lead directly to the Serenity plantation and observed the sign over the entranceway which read, "Welcome to all who enter Jebediah's Serenity."

"That's the first thing I'm getting rid of," mumbled Jameson as he pulled the coach up close enough to reach the sign and unhook it. "That will make good kindling for our fist fire," he said as he and threw it angrily into the dirt.

The grounds were completely overgrown. Obviously, no had been living there for quite some time and they could not be sure if it was safe to take up residence. Jameson noticed a paper nailed to one of the posts which he grasped and ripped off the pole. It was deteriorated and yellowed but he could make out the vague image on the poster and the writing. He was surprised to see it was an artist's rendition of him and the print read:

"Jameson Hartford....Wanted for crimes against the Confederacy including murder and treason…One thousand dollars reward… Dead or Alive."

He was perplexed as he crumpled up the paper which fell apart in his hands as he let it scatter on the ground, preferring not to mention this disturbing event to Delilah.

Jameson decided they should travel to Willow Hills and spend the night in a hotel, that is, if the town was still there. Again, they set off for the next location, traveling quickly and carefully through the tree covered and moss strewn roadway. A little further down the road their trip was deterred by a large dead tree which blocked the path forcing them to take a detour into town. This would be the longer route but would allow them to see the condition of other plantations.

After much maneuvering to avoid huge holes in the road and piles of debris, there in the distance lay the stately White Tranquility plantation. Jameson remembered it well from his days in South Carolina but did not know the proprietor, Grayson "Grady" Whitney, very well as he tended to keep to himself. Delilah could only recall tales of cruelty she had heard from other slaves she had encountered.

Grady was a nickname for his given name of Grayson. It was a family name handed down from generation to generation as far back as anyone could remember. All first born males of the Whitman family were christened Grayson.

The problem was that Grady was a twin, so his father named both boys Grayson, but gave them a different middle name so they could distinguish between the identical brothers. One was named Grayson

Charles, the other Grayson Davis. They were each known by two names until they went to school where they were given the nicknames of Gray C and Gray D which were quickly mashed together to be Gracie and Grady. To further distinguish themselves, Gracie always wore black while Grady was always in white.

Grayson Charles, his wife and 2 sons were killed by the advancing Northern army as they tried to mount an offense against them. Grayson Davis was smarter than, or perhaps not as brave as his brother, and hid with his wife and daughter; his sons were already fighting for the "cause" and two of them would pay the ultimate price.

White Tranquility was a medium sized plantation, fundamentally untouched by the invading Yankees. Yes it was ransacked and anything of value was taken, but Grady was clever and stashed many of his treasures inside hidden wall panels well before the pillagers arrived. Luckily they did not burn it or knock it down. This was not the case with the majority of properties in the area. The Yankees had no sympathy for the Rebels and looted and burned most of the other plantations.

White Tranquility stood large and proud, snow white in color with white shutters and a full wraparound porch. It was in need of some repair but there was nothing a good painting and some expert carpentry would not cure.

Grady wanted to rebuild it and restore it to its former glory but he had no money. Like all other true southerners, he converted all his currency into confederate dollars which were now totally worthless.

He did not appear to be biased, but he truly was, from his silver white hair and stubbly beard to his white waistcoat, trousers, shoes and hat. His clothing suited his bias to a tee.

Grady originally had three sons and one daughter, but again like all the other southern families, the able bodied boys went off to war and sadly only one returned; the eldest, appropriately named, Grayson Junior. Grady senior's limp kept him from being drafted, so he reluctantly stayed behind.  He had broken his leg when he accidentally fell off his horse chasing some runaways and was dragged for about a mile before the horse was encouraged to stop. The bones and ligaments were torn beyond repair, so he inherited a permanent limp.

Grady swore revenge against all northerners for his loss and was still holding the grudge even though the war was over. He was not about to concede to anything the north decreed and would try to keep the southern world he knew alive and well.


As Jameson, Delilah and their coach approached the plantation, they were surprised to see black men laboring in the fields which prompted them to stop and inquire as to their status. One of the men looked up, and was shocked to see a black woman riding in a coach next to a white man and dressed so fine.

He said, "Mista Whitney don't like us talkin' to strangers. We'll get punished, so please let us be."

Delilah answered, "Are you people still in slavery?"

"Yes'm," he said as if that was a ridiculous inquiry.

"Don't you know, you are free? You are all free! The war is over!"

"Don't know nothin' bout that ma'am. Got to get back to work."

Shocked, she looked at Jameson who also had a puzzled expression on his face.

Nanny's voice came from inside the coach, "They don't know they're free? Somebody set these poor people straight."

Before any further conversation could ensue Grayson Whitney junior came running up to the coach and shouted, "Get out of here, you're trespassing on private property. I'll shoot you if I have to."

Junior was a strapping young man, who was the spitting image of his father. He even held grudges against all northerners and all blacks, blaming them for the deaths of his brothers, relatives and his beloved southern way of life, instead of attributing his losses to his own racism and stubbornness.

Delilah screamed at him, "Don't these people know they are free? Did you not tell them President Lincoln freed all of them? Don't you know the war is over? What is wrong with you?"

Jameson tried to calm her down, but she was fuming.

A loud gunshot shook everyone into silence as the elder Whitney approached the wagon.

"Get out of here, now!" he demanded.

"How dare you tell us to leave," Delilah started up again.

Jameson whispered, "Lilah, we're on their land, let's not get shot before we have a chance to help everyone. Let me try to handle the situation."

She reluctantly agreed.

Mister Whitney, I'm Jameson Hartford from the Serenity plantation back down the road."

"I heard all about you Hartford. You caused a lot of trouble in these parts years ago. I don't want to hear anything you have to say. Get out!"

"Well you better listen, because these people are free and you are breaking the law by not telling them they are free and keeping them in bondage."

"Look, Hartford, I don't owe you or anybody else an explanation but let me tell you so you can understand; I lost everything in the war, I have no money and I need my crops planted and tended to so I can sell them and feed my family. My son and I cannot do it alone, so who really cares if a few coloreds are still forced to work for me for a little while."

"Who cares? Who cares? I'll tell you who cares. They care and so do I and so do all the thousands of soldiers who gave their lives so all people could be free," Delilah screamed, as she tried to jump off the wagon but was restrained by her cautious husband.

"Mister Whitney, you know I'm right and you have no jurisdiction over these people. Free them now or I will have the authorities come and force you to free them and arrest you, then none of your crops will planted or picked."

"Don't you understand, Hartford, I need them to do the work."

"Then hire them and pay them as you would any worker.'"

"I don't have the money to pay anyone."

Jameson whispered something to Delilah. She nodded in the affirmative as he turned to Grady, "We returned to this area to help in the rebuilding and reclamation of the land. We are willing to give you a loan so you can hire people to work on your plantation and pay them a fair living wage, but first you will have to tell these people they are free and let them decide if they wish to work here or not. The choice is yours."

"If you have money, why would you come back here?"

"I want to help my people," Delilah said enthusiastically.

Grady thought about it for a second and realized he really had no choice, so he agreed, much to the chagrin of his son, who was willing to fight rather than succumb to these northerner's demands.

Grady tried to calm him down saying, "We have to pick and choose our fights these days son and this is one we cannot win."

Then he leant in and whispered in his ear, "At least not right now."

The boy grinned and they both reluctantly agreed. The workers were told of their rights. At first they were dumbfounded and could not believe it. They thought it was some sort of trick, but after being reassured by Delilah, they began whooping and hollering. They could hardly believe it and praised God for their freedom. They thanked the Hartford's, ran for their meager possessions and quickly left the plantation before Grady and his son could offer them paying jobs.

The two Whitman's looked at Jameson and Delilah and said, "Now what? I have no workers and no money. What do you have to say to that? This better work out or we're gonna even the score with your lives."

Jameson said they would be addressing the town tomorrow and would have the money wired into the bank in a day or two. He would keep them informed.

"You better not cross me, Hartford," Grady threatened.

"Mister Whitney, how did you manage to hide the fact from your slaves that they were free? Didn't the union army tell them they were free when they came through these parts?"

"The damn Yankees told them and they all ran off. As soon as the army was long gone, we went after them and rounded them up again, at least the ones we could find. We told them the north lost the war and they had to come back, they had no choice. Besides, they had nowhere else to go, no food, no money, no education, what else could they do to feed their families?" Grady said laughing.

Delilah was fuming and ready to change her mind about the loan as Jameson quickly started the horses for Willow Hills

"See you soon, Hartford," Grady yelled.

"I can't believe him. How could someone still have slaves, James? What is wrong with these people?"

"You can't change an ingrained way of life so easily, I guess, even one that is so abhorrent."

"We will, my love, we will," she stated very confidently.

Meanwhile the Whitney's were debating what to do if the money did not come. Murder was one solution junior quickly announced. The elder Grady only smiled and said, "In the meantime son, let's go round up those workers of ours and get a few more days of free labor."


Driving the carriage for another few miles they discovered a lot of destroyed property and abandoned houses. They wondered what had become of the people and grew increasingly concerned as to what they would find when they eventually made it to Willow Hills.

As they turned around the next bend, they spied a clearing and set back, a ways off the main road, was a makeshift village of tents, covered wagons and lean-tos; a shanty town filled with poor black people.

Jameson noted, "This must be where the poor people, who were freed, are trying to survive. Look at these deplorable conditions and such substandard housing."

"Maybe we should stop and ask them about the poor woman and Ruby Rose," Delilah said.

Before they could make a decision, their carriage was spotted and a large group of people charged the unsuspecting visitors screaming, "Get them; get their carriage and horses. Stop them, don't let them get away."

"That doesn't sound like a welcoming committee."

Jameson hit the reins on the horses and shouted "Get going."

The horses progressed into a gallop as they desperately tried to out run the unruly mob.

"Hold on in there," Jameson screamed to the occupants of the coach as he tried to outrun their pursuers.

Nanny, Dawnalee and Ruby Rose were jostled back and forth as the dust kicked up by the horses found its way inside the carriage and forced them to not only try to remain seated, but to cough uncontrollably.

One man managed to get close enough and grab a hold onto the coach step. From there he tried to boost himself up and seized Delilah's leg. Jameson struck him with the butt of his rifle until he released his hold. Then he fired his gun into the air which seemed to frighten the mob if only for a moment allowing them to pull away.

As they sped further down the road and crossed a small bridge, they noticed the mob stopped chasing them, as if they were afraid to come any further. Perhaps this was a dividing line and they were forbidden from approaching any closer to the town limits. For the moment, they appeared to be safe and able to continue their journey at a safer speed.

The next turn brought them into Willow Hills. The town had not changed much, various buildings of different size and structure lined both sides of the dirt road. It was not as badly burnt and bombed as they had expected, though a lot of the buildings were deserted and closed for business. Everyone in the street stopped to look at these newcomers. They were eyed with fear and skepticism. A white man and a colored woman together, in their town; they would have to check into this matter immediately.

Right there as you entered the town was the hangman's gallows. A black person was left dangling there perhaps as a warning to the others to stay away.

"Isn't it a pity, it appears as if nothing is different here," Jameson sighed.

"We will change that," said Delilah defiantly.

Jameson noticed that Taffeta Jones Gentleman's Entertainment Emporium was open and still standing; obviously even the Yankees enjoyed a night at Taffy's and decided to spare it.

As they rode past the doctor's office, they noticed old Doctor Robert Pritchard was still practicing there. Jameson called to him. He emerged from his office looking a lot older and much more tired than they remembered him. The war took a toll on everyone, especially doctors. *"He must be at least 70 by now,"* Jameson thought as he watched the man who had delivered him walk slowly up to the coach. He was stunned to see them; but instead of a warm welcome, he delivered them a stern warning.

"Jameson Hartford, is that you? You shouldn't have come back, Jameson. People here blame you for the war and the death of their loved ones."

"Is that any way to greet an old friend?"

They embraced, but Doc once again warned Jameson to be careful. Then he recognized another one of his patients.

"Good day to you, Delilah, isn't it? You look so different since the last time I saw you. You look … very lovely, yes very pretty indeed. How are you?"

"I'm fine doctor. Thank you. We're married and we have a little girl now."

Doc peered into the carriage and said, "I see, she is beautiful, like her mother. Hello there little one, oh and hello to Nanny too, how are you my dear woman?"

"I'm fine doctor, just fine, thank you. It's good to see you again too."

Delilah smiled, and said, "We're going to try to build some businesses and a school to help my people, actually to help everyone, if they'll let us."

"Well this town needs help; a lot of help. The war all but destroyed the will of these folks to survive. I hope they'll let you help them. Good luck to you with that. Been some changes since you were last here, be careful; both of you."

"We will doctor, we will. See you later. When we have Serenity up and running again, we'll have you over for dinner, okay?"

Doc nodded, "I can't wait for a Nanny cooked meal again: it's been way to long."

"Then it is a date, doctor."

Doc went back into his office and Jameson headed to the hotel. They would spend the night in town, if at all possible.

At first, the proprietor balked and did not want colored people in his hotel, but the lure of the rare Yankee dollars quickly changed his mind and he eagerly grabbed the legal tender from Jameson's hand. Jameson acquired 2 rooms in the hotel and unloaded his belongings, telling Nanny and the two children to remain in the room, he and Delilah were going to see the banker and arrange for funds to be transferred. The sooner they attended to their business, the better.

As they passed by the sheriff's office, they were stopped by Mordechai Le Brute, the new sheriff.

"They made you sheriff?" Jameson said in disbelief.

Mordechai Le Brute was the captain of a slave ship, until it was outlawed and then began to run the slave auctions in Charleston. He made a living buying and selling human flesh. He was still a husky bearded man with a patch over one eye, but this time he had a tin star pinned to his chest. He wore a Stetson hat with a suede vest over his tan shirt, blue jeans and cowboy boots. Perhaps he had read too many western novels.

"I can't believe they elected you sheriff."

"Tough times call for tough leadership, uh Jameson Hartford, isn't it? I never thought I'd see you again."

"Well, uh sheriff, let's see how good you are at your job. I have the remains of a young black woman I found on the side of the road, in my coach here. She was tarred and feathered. Do you know anything about that?"

"It did not happen here. We don't allow that sort of thing in my town."

"We saw what kind of justice you dole out, back at the gallows."

"That's only to keep the peace. We can't have lawlessness, now can we? That woman was probably the victim of a vigilante group. There are a lot of them around the area, like Randall's Raiders. They are a group of confederate soldiers who don't believe the war is over and go around dispensing their own brand of justice; can't do anything about that. Besides, there is a food shortage around here due to the Yankees and people are very protective of what they have. She is an unfortunate statistic."

"An unfortunate statistic, is that what you call the death of a human being? Did you know her little child was there and saw the whole thing? I want those people found and punished," Delilah screamed.

"I'm sorry for the child but I can't do that. I am only one person and there are at least a dozen of them. Besides nobody knows where they go or when they will strike again. You just stay out of their way if you want to survive."

"So you won't do anything?"

"I don't think I can do very much."

"What you mean is that you don't want to do anything. Isn't that correct? Are you only the sheriff of the white people or of all people? We want to see to her final needs and will pay to have her properly buried in the town cemetery."

"I'm afraid that can't be done."

"What do you mean?"

"The townspeople won't allow a negro to be buried in their cemetery."

"How can that be? Don't they know the war is over and we are all free now?"

"Calm down, miss, you're in the south now, some traditions don't die easily."

"Tradition…is that what you call bigotry now? I won't stand for it, do you hear me?"

Mordechai looked at Jameson and said, "Can't you control your wife, she is causing a spectacle in the street?"

"He does not control me. I am not his property, I am his wife and I will speak up as I please. And from now on you will refer to me as Mrs. Hartford. Do you understand?"

Mordechai was embarrassed and wanted to resolve this matter as quickly as possible.

"Look, I misspoke, please come inside and we'll fill out the necessary forms for the US army to follow up on, OK?"

Mordechai led them into his office where they witnessed the jail cells in the back room full of people, black people; crammed into a small space without food or water; no room to even lie down.

"What is this?" demanded Delilah.

"These people were caught trying to steal food from the store. I had to arrest them."

"That's not true," yelled one of the prisoners, "they won't sell us any food. Our women and children are starving. They won't let us work, unless we become their slaves again. We have no money; so we have no choice but to take the food if we want to live."

"Shut up in there," Mordechai demanded.

"We are going to change all of this," Delilah emphatically stated.

"Let them go, Mordechai," Jameson said.

"They owe money for the damage they did."

"How much?"

"Ten, no twenty dollars….American not Confederate."

"Here," Jameson reached into his pocket, produced the required amount and demanded they all be set free.

Mordechai unlocked the cell and the former prisoners filed past their two liberators, thanking them as they went.

"You all be good now and obey the laws," Mordechai shouted after them. "Return yourselves to Black Woods and stay there." He looked at Jameson and added, "Unfortunately they will be back;" they have nothing. We need to clean that place out once and for all."

"Why don't you help them instead?" Jameson inquired.

"Don't worry we will help them," stated Delilah.

"I still want that complaint filled out," said Jameson.

As the prisoners started to leave, another figure entered the jail house. He looked at Delilah, took her hand, kissed it and said, "Never have I seen such a beautiful golden lady. I have been with many women but you Mademoiselle are by far the prettiest. I would be honored to take you to dinner tonight."

Delilah was flattered by the attention from this suave, handsome, finely dressed gentleman with the French accent and small pencil thin mustache, wearing a belt with a dueling sword hung at his side. In fact, she blushed at all the attention.

Jameson was quick to jump in and add, "This is my wife you are talking to sir. I don't appreciate the liberties you are taking."

"Pardon me, monsieur, but I did not know she was married. That is such a pity."

Mordechai interrupted, "This is my half-brother, Michelle. He is visiting me from New Orleans. He is a bit of a ladies man, besides," he whispered, "he was also a former pirate running illegal goods and rum down there through all the bayous, eluding the law very effectively I might add. Michelle, this is Jameson Hartford and his wife Delilah."

"I am pleased to make your acquaintance," Michelle said, but he did not take his eyes off Delilah the whole time. "Madam, pardon the liberty but you should let your hair grow, and you would look more ravishing than you do now."

Delilah had kept her hair short from the days when she worked on the plantation. Jameson had always told her how much he loved her hair cut real short so she kept it that way for him all these years. Now, suddenly she was having second thoughts.

"Watch yourself, Le Brute," Jameson again stated.

"I assure you my good man, that if she wanted me as much as I want her, there is little you could do about it."

Jameson was getting infuriated when Mordechai interfered and tried to calm things down, pushing Michelle into the office and Jameson and Delilah out onto the street.

"Do not underestimate his skills, Mister Hartford, my brother is a master swordsman and should not be trifled with. I will take care of this," he assured them.

"You better," threatened Jameson.

When they had gone, Mordechai turned to Michelle and said, "That one is big trouble brother, leave them both alone."

Michelle responded, "I can take care of him, and I will have his beautiful wife; mark my words."

Mordechai glared at his brother and said, "Michelle do not start any trouble again, do you hear me? I won't be able to save you every time. I am the sheriff here; I have a responsibility to this town and all the people here. I'm warning you to behave and stay away from that woman."

"Don't worry my brother, I won't start anything, but if she desires me, what can I do? I will have to oblige her, no?"

"Do you remember the day you came here and begged for my help? Do you? Well let me remind you."

It was just a little over a year ago when Michelle LeBrute slipped into town and asked his brother to hide him. He was being chased by a jealous husband's brother. Back in New Orleans, he had seduced the poor man's wife and then once he had succeeded in his conquest demanded that she should pay for Michelle's silence, when she refused, he had the audacity to tell her husband. The man was so mad he left his wife and threatened to kill Michelle. The wily Frenchman slew him first, then when the law drew too close, he ran to the only safe haven he could find, Willow Hills, South Carolina. He was trailed by the dead husband's brother who had enlisted the help of an army unit, led by a Lieutenant Wellington. They were charged with traveling from town to town in an effort to keep the peace in the south after the Civil War.

This was not Michelle's first offense as he was adept at being a gigolo, preying upon wealthy lonely women. When he grew tired of them or they grew weary of supporting him, he would eagerly find another willing benefactor. He thought nothing of destroying people's lives for his own satisfaction and leaving them in ruin. Mordechai understood from the Lieutenant that at least three of these scorned ladies had committed suicide rather than face their shame, yet it meant nothing to Michelle, he just continued in his nefarious ways. Two others threatened to go to the authorities and were summarily dispatched with a stab wound to their chest. The murder weapon could not be located and, until now, there were no clues. Then a tenacious dead husband's brother was able to connect the dots, fill in the missing clues and informed the law of the wily Frenchman with the sword.

Lieutenant Wellington and the brother-in-law trailed Michelle to the forlorn southern town, where Mordechai was forced to lie for his brother and swore he knew not where his brother was and hadn't heard from him in years. In return, Michelle promised never to do it again, yet he could not seem to control himself as lonely ladies from neighboring towns continued to succumb to his charms and fall victim to his evilness. Each time he begged his brother for forgiveness and vowed that it would be the last time.

Lieutenant Wellington suspended the investigation when the brother-in-law turned up missing and could not be found. Mordechai had his suspicions but could not prove his brother had done away with the man in order to have the inquiry dropped, due to lack of an eyewitness. The lieutenant had no idea what Michelle looked like and besides he was more interested in spending time at Taffy's emporium with his men and in eating, drinking and partaking of the lovely ladies all gratis, or for his "protection" as he so eloquently referred to it. Just another corrupt person seeking to take advantage of the war ravaged south. He remained in town availing himself of whatever he pleased until new orders arrived and he and his men were forced to leave. Mordechai wanted to stop them but feared they would renew their quest for his brother, so he tolerated their abuse of his town and its people.

"Do you remember? I will never forget and now here you are again trying to seduce another woman. This one is trying to rebuild and save this sad excuse for a town and I will not stand for it this time."

"Relax, my brother, I am only toying with her, I will not do anything, alright? Have I laid your fears to rest?"

Mordechai had his doubts and just watched as his half-brother sauntered out of the office with that familiar smirk on his face.

Jameson and Delilah started back to the hotel, but a question plagued her, "James, what will we do with the poor woman's body?"

"I guess we will bring it back to Serenity with us and bury her there."

'We are going to have to change a lot of minds around here. I don't think it will be as easy as I had hoped."

"We'll do what we can, darling, that's all anyone can expect."

Some stragglers, soldiers returning from the war, were dragging themselves down the street, hoping to find their homes and loved ones after fighting in the horrific war. Delilah recognized one of the men as a person who had mistreated her when she was a slave.

She ran up to him, looked into his hollowed out eyes and scrawny frame, and asked him, "Do you know who I am?"

He glanced up at her and replied, "I'm afraid I do not. Should I?"

"You don't remember the face of a woman you abused these many years ago?"

"I regret I do not."

"You can't hurt me anymore, but I can destroy you if I want. How does that make you feel?"

"If I hurt you I am sorry. There is no excuse for what I did. I can only ask for your forgiveness, ma'am."

Delilah wanted to yell at him further and hurt him the way he hurt her, but he was so pathetic looking, so frail; she supposed he already went through hell and nothing she could do would be any worse than what he had already experienced.

"I can forgive you, but I can never forget," she responded.

"Thank you ma'am, I don't deserve even that but I am truly sorry."

He continued on his way and she rejoined Jameson as together they returned to the hotel.


Meanwhile a mob was beginning to form with murmurings of the extraordinary couple and the trouble and deaths that had occurred the last time they were in South Carolina. Some even recalled a wanted poster and reward on the man but were unsure of the details and no one had a copy of the old careworn poster. They all agreed that they wanted justice, or their form of justice, and would settle for nothing less. They made their way to the sheriff's office to inquire of the two strangers and what they were doing in their town. They mistrusted all strangers, especially northerners. They wanted answers or a riot would commence.

# Chapter 3

## *Reunions*

Jameson, Delilah, Nanny, Dawnalee and Ruby Rose were resting comfortably in their hotel room, discussing their plans and the new businesses they would start when a knock on the door interrupted their thoughts.

"Who is it?" asked Jameson

"It is Sheriff Le Brute, open the door please."

Jameson thinking that the sheriff had brought the necessary complaint papers for him to sign opened the door only to find another surprise.

"I regret to have to do this, but you are under arrest for the murders of all those people at your plantation four years ago. You are a wanted man and there is a bounty on your head. I do not have a choice. Here look at this."

Sheriff Le Brute produced a time worn yellowed poster, the same one Jameson had seen tacked to the fence at his plantation earlier that day.

"What? That is ridiculous. Those people were trespassing on my property and came to kill me, I was only defending myself."

Delilah grabbed the poster, scanned it and echoed her husband's protest.

"Nevertheless you will have to stand trial," LeBrute said apologetically.

"Trial…by whom? Is there a judge in this sad excuse for a town?"

"We will have to wait for a circuit judge to arrive."

"And you plan on keeping me locked up until then?"

"Unless you can meet bail."

"So that's it. You want money. This is so pitiful."

"Please come along quietly, Mister Hartford."

"I'll take good care of your wife in your absence," said Michelle.

"You keep your hands off her or I'll kill you."

"That is a very incriminating remark, monsieur."

"I'll be right there with the bail money, James, don't worry," said Delilah.

Mordechai took Jameson as Michelle eyed Delilah. She looked at him with a glint of a smile on her face and closed the door before he could say or do anything further.

"I don't like that man. He's trouble. Stay away from him Miss Delilah," said Nanny.

"I need the money in the suitcase to bail James out."

She rummaged through the clothes, finding the envelope and a stash of cigars. She took one out, bit off the end and struck a match, igniting it. She took a large puff, inhaled it and exhaled releasing a large plume of smoke. She grabbed the money and left the room.

Out on the street, she was the victim of rude stares and unkind whispers, none of which bothered her, until she ran into Abigail and her sister Annabelle. Abigail was Jameson's first wife whom he divorced to marry Delilah. Annabelle had always had designs on her sister's husband and still did. This time the difference was staggering. Delilah was dressed in the finest clothes, while the two sisters had to be satisfied with their old outdated tattered outfits. How ironic, that the first time they had all met Delilah was in rags and Abigail and Annabelle were in the latest fashions. How times had changed. Delilah wore a light green dress that clung to her perfectly contoured body like it was painted on, while Abigail and Annabelle were dressed in blue and tan gowns that were in fashion four years ago. Their bonnets, shoes and purses were old, scuffed and worn. They stared daggers at each other, until Abigail broke the silence.

"Is Jameson here? How is he? Is he ok? Where is he? I want to see him."

"He's fine. We're very happy."

"I didn't ask about you, I don't care about you. I don't even remember your name, not that it's important."

"My name is Mrs. Hartford, Mrs. Delilah Hartford. You would do well to remember it."

"I'll never call you that. You'll always be the slut who stole my husband."

"I didn't steal your husband, your lies and incriminating actions gave him to me."

"Look, she smokes a cigar," Annabelle laughed, "how uncouth, no class at all."

Delilah took a large puff on the cigar inhaled it and blew it defiantly into Annabelle's face, forcing her to cough uncontrollably. Delilah then stared at Abigail who became frightened, moved quickly out of the way and allowed Delilah to proceed to the sheriff's office. If looks could kill, Abigail and Annabelle would have slain Delilah right there on the spot, glaring at her as she strode away down the road shaking her derriere in defiance.

Delilah posted the required bail and Jameson was set free, but he was warned not to leave the area. This would calm the crowd for a while and satisfy their many and varied wrongful grudges.

Delilah led Jameson across the street so as not to run into the two sisters. This route took them directly in front of Taffeta Jones Gentleman's Emporium.

As they passed, Jameson couldn't help but look inside at the long polished wood bar with brass rails, the crystal chandeliers, the scent of beer and whiskey permeating the air and the scantily clad women; oh those promiscuous wenches. They heard cries coming from a corner table and a voice that sounded all too familiar. Jameson and Delilah entered to find Madeline, Jebediah's wife, posing as a saloon girl. She was trying to fend off an over-eager customer clad in a confederate uniform sporting a curious double R patch on both arms.

"Please sir, stop it. I'm not that kind of girl."

"Come here honey, I'll make you that kind of girl."

"Stop it sir."

"Don't tell me to stop it. I'm paying good money here, I want you," the soldier said as he slapped her across the face.

Taffy stepped in and said, "That's enough! Let her be. She is not one of those girls. I'll get you one of my special women."

"I want this woman… and I always get what I want."

Taffeta Jones was a shrewd businesswoman. She was always dressed to the nines and looked no different today. A luxurious low cut red gown, painted face, red lips, hair swept up upon her head and a husky sexy voice. She would try to change the soldier's mind with her wiles.

"Come on now, do you want someone who is naive or someone seasoned in pleasuring a gentleman such as yourself?"

The soldier pushed her out of the way and grabbed Madeline.

"I'll show her all she needs to know."

Jameson entered the conversation much to Taffy's amazement, "Sir, that girl is my niece and I've come to take her home. Please let her go. I'll pay for you to enjoy another lady, alright?"

"Uncle Jameson, Aunt Delilah, what are you doing here? I'm so ashamed; I don't want you to see me like this."

She grabbed her shawl and tried unsuccessfully to cover herself up.

"You want her, Yankee, you fight for her."

"I'm no Yankee, sir, I was born right here in South Carolina. I would rather settle this like gentlemen. There is no need for violence."

"I like violence, and I'm no gentleman."

"Please sir, I don't want any trouble."

Too bad, you already got it," the soldier said as he charged at Jameson, pushing him through the doors and into the street.

Michelle was following Delilah and saw this as a chance to impress her. He demanded the fight stop immediately and pulled the two men apart.

"Michelle, I can handle this," claimed Jameson.

"Michelle, Michelle, what kind of name is that? Did your parents want a girl?" the soldier snickered.

"You have insulted me. I challenge you to a duel."

Michelle pulled out his glove and slapped the surprised soldier across the face.

"A duel? With swords? Hell no, I don't duel, I'm just gonna shoot you."

The soldier reached for his gun, but Michelle, being a champion swordsman, pulled his weapon from its scabbard at lightning speed and struck the soldiers hand, knocking the gun loose and slicing off a bit of his hand. The furious soldier screamed and charged at Michelle who raised his sword and stabbed the man straight through his abdomen. Michelle knew precisely where to place his blade to exact the kind of wound he wanted. He could either impose a slight wound, a deep gash, or death; the decision was his to make.

The soldier fell to the ground gasping out his last breaths. Michelle stood proudly atop his prey and cleaned off his blade on the soldier's jacket. Mordechai was not exaggerating about his brother. He was fast and accurate with his sword. Jameson and Delilah were astonished at his quickness.

Michelle quickly bowed toward Delilah and said, "I saved your husband for you. Perhaps he is not worthy of such a fine woman as yourself."

Jameson was about to challenge him when Mordechai came running over.

"What happened here?"

"I had to kill him brother, it was self-defense."

The others all nodded in agreement.

"Do you know who that is?"

"A nameless drunk, who did not deserve to live?"

"No my brother, see that patch on his arm, the double R, he is a member of Randall's Raiders, the rebel group who think the war is not over. They are renegades who run rampant throughout the area, enforcing their own laws and killing anyone who dares to disagree with them. You have made a bad enemy. They will come looking for you."

"I am not afraid, I can handle myself," Michelle boasted as he smiled at Delilah.

Jameson walked over to Delilah and Madeline and said, "C'mon let's get out of here."

Madeline was still a southern belle even after all she had been through. She was still beautiful and polite and worried as much about other people as she did about herself. She was working in Taffy's so she had to be a "painted lady" in a low cut dress to entice the customers, but that was not like her at all.

Delilah asked, "Madeline, why are you working in a saloon?"

"Oh Aunt Delilah, I'm so embarrassed. After the fire at the plantation, Jeb and I had to recuperate; I had a broken leg and he was badly burnt. We eventually rebuilt the plantation and were going to live there until the Confederate army came and arrested Jeb for desertion. They took him away. I had no visible means of support. I couldn't locate my family and came into town looking for employment, but because of the war, jobs were scarce, no one wanted to hire me. Miss Taffy heard of my plight and offered me a position in her saloon. I told her I could not be one of her mistresses and she said all I had to do was entertain the guests, get them to buy more drinks and lure them into the casino to gamble away their fortunes. If they wanted more, she would have one of the other girls oblige. I had no choice but to accept."

"There's no shame in that Madeline. We all do what we must do to survive," said Delilah.

"Madeline, is the plantation habitable?" asked Jameson

"Yes, it should be Uncle Jameson, unless someone ransacked it. It was in perfect condition, fully furnished, when I left. Will you be going back there?"

"We plan to go tomorrow morning. You are more than welcome to come with us."

"Oh, I'd love to, thank you so much, but I have to tell Miss Taffy."

"You two go back to the hotel, I'll square things up with Taffy and join you in a minute," replied Jameson.

"I'm so happy to see both of you. I haven't heard a word about Jeb, I fear he's dead."

"Come along Madeline, I'll tell you a story about Jeb."

Jameson went into the saloon and spoke to Taffy, who was happy to see him again, probably one of the only townsfolk to feel that way. She embraced him and politely kissed him on the cheek. He returned the kiss. Jameson told her he would be moving back to Serenity and about Delilah's plans to help her people. Taffy was most congenial and offered to help in any way she could. She was that kind of lady.

"Jameson, the man Michelle killed, his army unit will come looking for him. They are dangerous, be sure you are in no way tied to that murder, okay?"

"I didn't kill him so there shouldn't be a problem."

"I don't trust the sheriff's brother, neither should you."

"I'll be careful, thank you Taffy."

"Come back any time Jameson, I'd like to but you a drink and discuss old times."

Jameson smiled as he left the saloon, but was quickly surprised by Abigail and Anabelle who had followed him there. He couldn't help but notice the changes in their attire and their faces. Abigail was the brunette and Annabelle the blonde, only their faces were careworn and their hair disheveled. They tried to maintain a stature of life that they were no longer a part of; it had died with the war.

"Abby, Belle, how are you?"

Annabelle ran up to him placed, her arms around him, tried to give him a great big kiss on the lips. He turned his head so it landed on his cheek.

Annabelle said, in her usual sing song voice, "I missed you Jameyson, so much."

"Oh Belle, please, grow up," he said as he pulled her arms loose and pushed her away.

"Well, is that any way to greet your sister-in-law?"

"Annabelle, please, act like a lady," Abigail stated.

"Well I never," she said indignantly.

Abigail turned toward Jameson and said, "Hello Jameson, I'm surprised to see you back in Willow Hills."

"Not any more surprised than I. We returned, uh Delilah and I, to try to help out. Where are you living? Is Tall Oaks still there?"

"Yes, the Yankees left it pretty much alone. I wish I could say the same for Annabelle and me, what with no man there to protect us, we were easy prey."

Jameson paused for a moment, then added, "I'm so sorry Abby. You could have stayed up north."

"We couldn't. I couldn't watch you being in love with that; well, what's done is done. We were all just trying to survive that horrible war. We belong here in the south; we're southern belles and always will be. The north is just so foreign to us. At least the soldiers gave us money so we could buy food and stay alive."

"We are going to live at Serenity again; if I can help you in any way, please let me know. I look forward to seeing you again."

"Oh Jameson, I have thought about you often and wondered if I would ever see you again. There is so much I want to say to you. I'm so sorry for what happened between us, I was only trying to do what I thought was right."

"Please Abby, don't go on, I'm married, happily married and I.."

"I know, but I have to tell you how much I still love…"

"Abby, I have to be going; it was nice to see you again. Goodbye."

Abigail was dismayed that her advances were rebuffed and sadly she acquiesced to her former husband's wishes, for the present anyway.

"I'm sure we will run into each other again, it's a small town. Come on Annabelle, we need to get home, before it gets dark. It's not safe after sunset any longer."

"Goodbye Jameyson, stop over anytime."

As Jameson watched them leave, sadness overtook him. He remembered the good days he and Abigail had shared; time had a way of erasing the bad memories. He wondered what life would have been like had he never left her. Would the remembrances be as fond if they had remained together? He was snapped back to reality as a man came running up to him.

"Are you Jameson Hartford? The sheriff told me I would find you in here."

"Yes, I'm him."

"I have a telegram for you."

Jameson took the paper, opened it and read the shocking message:

"This is to inform you that one, Jebediah Hartford, has escaped our custody and feared headed in your direction. **STOP** Please exercise extreme caution as he has vowed revenge against you. **STOP** Alert appropriate authorities in your district at once.

Regards,

Captain Rollins, Boston Police Department, Massachusetts"

"Any reply sir?"

"No, not at this time, thank you."

Jameson wandered back to the hotel muttering, "Here we go again, the same old problems" and wondering if he should tell the ladies, about this odd turn of events. He would like to spare them the bad news but, it would be better for everyone's safety if they kept their eyes open and watched for any suspicious activities. Besides it would make Madeline happy. He decided to convey the contents of the telegram to all concerned, after dinner.

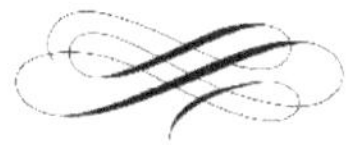

# Chapter 4

# *Return to Serenity*

The next morning, Jameson left the hotel early and walked briskly toward the bank. He was watched suspiciously as he strode down the street. He heard whispers and could see the fingers being pointed in his direction, but he paid it no mind. The bank building was a shell of its former self. No customers were inside and only one sole person appeared to be working there. The proprietor was a thin man, very nervous and balding. He had heard about this northerner who had returned to his roots and wondered like the rest of Willow Hills, what his true intentions were. Jameson instructed the banker that he and his wife would be depositing a large sum of money wired from Boston and would be funding a school, new construction and several new businesses. He hoped he would be able to help the local economy and provide jobs and income for the populace. The man was ecstatic not only for the deposit and business but for the impending industrial revolution, which would hopefully increase his business. He shook Jameson's hand, thanked him over and over and would not release his grip until he was sure Jameson was sufficiently acknowledged. Jameson departed and returned to the hotel amid the continuing stares and whispers.

Delilah had been thinking and decided that they should buy some food and provisions for the poor people in Black Woods. Those people desperately needed help right away. Jameson was apprehensive as he remembered their first encounter, but he finally agreed, with one caveat that they went alone, and left the children with Madeline. Nanny should come as she might be able to calm the situation, should it get out of hand.

They proceeded to the general store and were astonished at the bare cupboards. There was a shortage of food here just as they had been led to believe. Delilah wasn't fazed and began to order everything she thought was necessary. The store clerks just looked at her.

"We don't serve your kind in this store."

"You don't want to make money, even from a "colored" woman?"

Jameson interjected, "We have money, United States currency, not confederate. If you don't want it, we'll go to Charleston and spend it."

"Let me see it."

The clerk's eyes widened as he saw the bills. "Look, they do have money, even gold coins; what would you like sir?"

"I'd like you to apologize to my wife and never refer to her as anything but ma'am."

"Yes, yes, of course. I'm so sorry ma'am; I didn't mean anything by it. Please excuse me, ma'am."

Delilah ignored him and proceeded to rattle off her list of all the items they wanted consisting of food, canned goods, clothing, blankets, pots, even candy for the young, etc. Other patrons were curious and asked them why they were buying so much. Delilah politely told them it was none of their business. They started to figure out that the two strangers must be buying supplies for the colored folks and began to complain that there would be no food left for them. The shopkeeper, eager to keep the peace was getting nervous. Jameson dispelled their fears by saying he would replenish supplies by going into Charleston, if necessary. They carried their bundles outside, filled up their coach until it was overflowing and hurriedly went on their way before the crowd became an angry mob.

As they passed the gallows, the carriage was halted as Jameson and Delilah ascended the stairs and cut down the body of the poor man who was left there to hang as an example and a deterrent. They wrapped the body in a blanket and placed it in the back of the coach next to the woman who had been tarred and feathered. They were hoping to take both bodies back to be buried with their friends or relatives.

"That horrendous structure needs to be torn down. It's a reminder of a sad past, which is now over."

"Let's hope it's over, Lilah."

"We'll make sure it is, James."

They quickly departed down the road as a suspicious horde watched them disappear from view, muttering to themselves as to what they should do with these outsiders.

They crossed the bridge and turned the coach directly toward Black Woods. The poor people did not know what to expect as no coach ever dared to willingly approach them before; but as soon as it came to a halt, the people rushed the unsuspecting passengers, pulling Jameson, Delilah and Nanny off the coach as they began to ransack the supplies. Jameson fired his gun into the air and screamed at them to stop.

Delilah and Nanny tried to calm them down, but they were hungry and scared, a deadly cocktail. Jameson was overpowered and disarmed.

As he lay on the ground one man pointed the gun at him and was ready to pull the trigger, was it not for Nanny who kept shouting, "Stop it! Stop it! We're your friends, not enemies. We brought you all this food and clothing. Don't kill the man who cared enough to risk his neck and come here. What's the matter with you? Y'all are acting like animals?"

The crowd grew quiet as Nanny and Delilah began to tell them who they were, why they had come back and their plans for starting businesses and giving them jobs and an education. Jameson was released and rose to his feet.

A voice from the rear cried out, "Are you the Delilah from the Hartford plantation?"

Delilah turned around to see a tall thin black woman with cold dark eyes, staring at her. She was just as suspicious as the others, weighing these three new arrivals carefully.

"Yes."

"Was your mother's name Leah?"

"Yes, yes it was."

"Well then, come over here. There's someone you should meet."

Delilah was stunned and curious as she made her way through the crowd to the tent where the thin lady led her. She looked at the man and woman standing outside the tent, then pulled the flap open and entered. There, was an old sickly lady lying on a bed of dried leaves.

"Come over here child and let me have a look at you. My eyes ain't what they used to be."

Delilah approached the old woman, tears welling up in her eyes then her voice cracked as she cried, "Mama, is it really you?"

She ran over and fell to her knees, hugging her mother and repeatedly kissing her.

Leah looked very old. Her skin had wrinkled and her scraggly grey hair was wound up in a bun on top of her head. Years of being a slave, working in the hot sun, in the fields, took a toll on a human being and made them look and feel far older than they were. Leah was no exception. Her eyes were bad and her body ached from the hard labor, yet somehow she managed to survive all these years and here she was, just waiting for her long lost daughter.

"I can't believe it's you mama. They told me you were dead."

"Oh my my, Delilah, it is you, I can't believe it. I thought I would never see my baby again."

They hugged and cried and hugged some more, then Leah said, "Where are my manners child, say hello to your brother and sister."

Delilah looked up at the only other two people in the room as they introduced themselves.

"Hello Delilah, I'm your sister, Ambrosia," said the tall thin girl with the large afro.

"And I'm your brother, Marcus," said a tall strapping young man with a cleanly shaved bald head.

Delilah rose up and they all hugged each other.

"Oh Mama, I want you to meet someone too…my husband." Delilah ran out of the tent, grabbed Jameson by the arm and pulled him inside and over to her mother. Jameson was as surprised as Delilah, amazed that her mother had stayed alive, and happy for his wife that they were united again.

"This is my husband James."

"A white man, my sweet lord, you married a white man?"

"Mama, he's a great man. We even have a little daughter, your granddaughter, Dawnalee. I'm Mrs. Delilah Hartford now."

"Hello Leah," Jameson said.

"Hartford, you married a Hartford? Do you know what those Hartford's did to us?"

"Mama, James is not like that. He freed me and all the other slaves on his plantation. He risked his life and all he owned for me and our people, I love him and he loves me."

Jameson added, "I'm not like the other people who live here. I love your daughter very much and always will."

"White man, I don't want to be related to no white man."

She thought for a moment and then added, "Did you say your name was Jameson Hartford?"

"Yes," he replied.

She spat on the ground in front of him and shouted, "Get out of my tent, go, now!"

"Mama, what's the matter, why did you do that?"

"Child, he the reason we're slaves. His mother, Missus Hartford was trying to help us escape, when you were just a lil baby in my arms. She had the whole route planned out, all the people who were going to help us, then he came into the house and found out about it. Missus Harford told him what was goin' on and he swore he wouldn't tell, but he musta, cause we were caught. He musta told his no good father about the escape and the route we was gonna follow so they could find us and take us back. That's when they beat me and took you away from me and sold us to different plantations, so we would never see each other again. He broke his promise and told his father about us, that's why we were captured. He's no good, I tell you, no good."

"Wait, that was you, and the little baby you held in your arms was Delilah? I recall that day."

Jameson remembered the impromptu meeting and how he found out that his mother was helping slaves to escape. He recollected the lady and the little baby she held tightly in her arms. He could see it as if it were yesterday. It was his epiphany, the day that changed his mind on slavery and the day he decided to try and end the unholy practice.

"Oh my God, I can't believe it, I first met you years ago when we were both children; but you have to trust me, I never said a word to my father. I'm not the reason you were recaptured."

"You're a liar, just like all white men."

"Delilah, I swear I never told anyone about the planned escapes. I can't even believe that was you and your mother that I met so many years ago, but I did not tell anyone."

Delilah took Jameson's hand and looked into his eyes. She knew he was telling the truth and tried to convince her mother.

"Mama, James would never do that, he's a good man. He even tried to help me find you."

Leah was getting very upset, shaking and raising her voice at the very thought of this white man being married to her daughter. They were all afraid something would happen to her as she grew more and more irate unable to catch her breath.

"James, let me try to talk to her. Wait outside for me."

Jameson reluctantly walked out of the tent but there were no friendly faces to be found there either. They were all suspicious of him, calling him names and purposely bumping into him to try and start a fight.

Nanny kept saying, "Mind your manners. Let him be."

A group of men approached him and told him they were going to kill him, as there were no good white men. They kept yelling obscenities at him, trying to get him to throw the first punch. He would not be that foolish, but he was getting apprehensive and wondered if he would get out of there alive. Suddenly, he was struck from the side and the power of the punch sent him to the ground. He tried to get up as three other men piled on top of him holding him down while a third placed his hands into Jameson's pockets and searched for his belongings. Jameson tried to fight back but was severely outnumbered.

Nanny was striking at the assailants and screaming, "Let him go, get off of him. He's trying to help you all, you bunch of fools."

The assailants found his money, gold coins, pocket watch and fob. They took his pistol and ammunition. When they were satisfied that he had nothing left to pilfer, they decided to finish him off so he could not press charges against them.

Two women pushed their way to the front and began pulling the men off of Jameson, yelling at them to stop.

"Get off of him. What is wrong with you? Leave him be."

When the pummeling was stopped and Jameson was finally able to see; he looked at his rescuers and suddenly remembered them.

"Azure, Sienna, is that you?"

"Yes, it's us, Mista Hartford; we could never forget you and Nanny too. You probably saved our lives that day. We were starving and that meal you gave us helped us to survive."

There in front of him were the two poor girls he tried to purchase from the then slave trader, Mordechai Le Brute. He had given them a home cooked meal, but was denied their purchase by a fear driven town. He hugged them and they returned the affection. Azure told the crowd that he was a good man and they should leave him alone. Jameson cleaned himself off and proceeded to describe what he and Delilah were going to do for them, even the ones who had just tried to kill him. He told the entire crowd that he would be hiring tomorrow and anyone interested would be paid a fair wage; money that would enable them to survive. He promised them an education and jobs. They were all very interested but skeptical of the white man.

Delilah finally emerged from the tent and said, "Let's leave; mama needs to rest and this whole ordeal has upset her. I asked her to come live with us but she said no. Your family and father-in-law were horrible people and she can't forget what they did to her."

"Maybe in time, she'll see I'm not that kind of man and she will come to like me and trust me."

Delilah shrugged and said, "I hope so."

"Now that you know she is here, you can come and see her anytime you want."

"Next time we'll bring Dawnalee with us. Maybe her little granddaughter can melt that heart and change her mind, we can at least try."

The men reluctantly returned what they had stolen including the horse and carriage. Jameson removed the body of the tarred and feathered woman he found the day before, as well as the man from the gallows. He asked if anyone knew either of them; they were identified. Delilah told them about Ruby Rose and that she was in their protection. A woman came forward and said the child had no known relatives and no one needed another mouth to feed while food was so scarce. Delilah said she and Jameson would take care of Ruby Rose and adopt her in as their own daughter. They left the other two bodies there for proper burial and returned to Willow Hills. They had to buy supplies for themselves, pick up the children and Madeline, and finally make the trek back to Serenity.

Delilah's brother and sister tried to convince their mother to go with Delilah to the plantation. They could live like kings there and take advantage of him the way their kind took advantage of us. Leah refused at first, but was persuaded to accept the proposal and not suffer any longer. She would not, however, acknowledge a Hartford as her daughter's husband. They planned on moving there the very next day and gathered their meager possessions in anticipation.

The trip to Serenity revealed a number of burned down plantations and a lot of vacant land suitable for planting and farming. The once majestic buildings now lay in ruins and the valuable land lie dormant. If the town needed food, all available land should be farmed. They could plant vegetables, fruit trees, potatoes, peanuts, as well as cotton and tobacco. There was no reason to waste the arable land. There were plenty of trees to start a lumber business and supply logs to rebuild needed housing, especially for all the newly freed people. They could spin the cotton into yarn and have a textile mill. They could tailor clothing from the cotton and supply it to the populace. The ideas for the future seemed endless and their spirits were high.

Over the next hill they could see the rebuilt plantation. Serenity looked almost the same as the old estate. It was white with huge columns supporting the front porch, large windows with black shutters, but somehow it felt different. Upon entering the front doors they could see the interior almost mirrored the former except everything was new. There was a library, but it was no longer full of books, they were lost in the fire and along with them went Jameson's past. Pictures and records were lost forever; there were no links to his ancestry, not one photograph remained. Now he knew how Delilah must have felt, never knowing your lineage, having no knowledge of where you came from. He felt a little lost and sorry for himself and for what his wife went through as well.

Nanny was also nostalgic, having lived a good portion of her life in the old house, but before she entered the new Serenity she had to attend to a heartbroken memory. Nanny, hand in hand with Delilah, went to the cemetery and cleaned off two graves that were very important to both of them, pulling the weeds and readjusting the crosses and markers. One was for Uncky, Nanny's love and Serenity house servant who was murdered by those opposed to Jameson freeing his workers. The other for Delilah's first child, Eve, who was murdered by the evil overseer and Bethany Sue, Jebediah's mother, because the unfortunate baby was the result of her husband's rape of an unwilling slave girl, who was then wrongly blamed for the affair.

They both mourned but would not let the feeling linger for too long; there was work to be done.

"Okay everyone, grab a dust rag and a mop and let's get to work," Nanny ordered.

Yes, it was covered in a layer of dust and needed to be cleaned, and with everyone pitching in, the task was completed quickly, even with Nanny's strict rules. The kitchen was equipped with pots, plates, and dinnerware all waiting to be used. The couches and beds were in excellent condition and just needed refreshing and a good airing out.

The children went exploring around their new home, looking in every closet, nook and cranny. They accidentally discovered a secret passage in one of the hall closets and, as children will do, they followed it. Eventually the channel brought them underground and outside to a spot in the barn. Amazed by this find they raced to tell their mother.

The adults were astounded by the discovery. Jameson's family had lived in this mansion for decades and, to his recollection, no one had ever mentioned a secret passage. Perhaps his mother had used it years earlier to hide slaves and help them escape. They all followed in unison through the tunnel and out into the barn, but along the way they discovered a small treasure chest. Jameson lifted it up and was going to bring it into the house for closer inspection when something else caught his eye. There in the corner of the barn was a lantern, matches, a bottle with water in it and food scraps, that could not be more than a day old. Someone was using this passage and gaining admittance into the house. Who in the world could it be? That would be the discussion at dinner that night. In the meantime, they decided to close it off and make it inaccessible. Whoever it was would surely come back and try to get into the house again, now it would be virtually impossible.

The grounds of Serenity were in bad shape. They were overgrown and would need every able bodied men to clear it, plant crops and tend the fields. Jameson hoped he could persuade people to come and work, providing them a decent wage and decent housing. The other problem was Jebediah, he had cleared a large tract of trees on the southwestern corner of the property. This, coupled with the fires the advancing Yankees had set, destroyed a large swath of trees and brush which inadvertently created a swamp, that continued to spread and grow, engulfing a few acres of his and adjoining properties. The trees had regrown but the once barren land had acquired a wetland that would not go away. He did not know how to remedy this situation, but would not worry about it now, as they had a lot of work ahead of them.

Nanny prepared a scrumptious meal and they all sat down to dinner. It was their first meal in their new house, and a most enjoyable one, but the hot topic was the secret passage. Madeline wondered if it was not the swamp monster. It was a local legend that was growing as more and more people swore they had seen it. A creature that walked like a human but lived in the swamp, and terrorized the locals, stealing food, chickens, cattle, whatever it wanted, and then mysteriously the bones were returned in a few days to the very spot where the animal was taken. They didn't believe it or maybe didn't want to, calling it a silly superstition; Nanny was not too sure. The children were told to only play in the yard and never wander into the woods or fields, just to be sure.

Their stomachs full and their heads filled with grandiose plans for the future, they decided the first step in that direction was a good night's sleep, so they all retired to bed. Luckily, the house had four bedrooms so each had their own room, the children shared one bed.

Jameson could not sleep and eagerly opened the chest he had come across in the passageway. He found it to be a brief history of his family tree; items that had been tucked away as if no one wanted them to be made public. Checking through old yellowed photos and lineage was no easy task. The paper crumbled easily in his fingers and he desperately wanted to know what it said. There was a sepia toned photo of his great-great grandfather alongside a picture of a black woman, who must have been a slave, but wait, no, she was holding a child, a little girl child. A few more family photos showed the girl growing up with the woman and Jameson's great-great grandfather. As the child became an adult, her name became visible on the back of one of the photos, as Perfidia Hartford. Jameson's jaw dropped open as he realized this was his great grandmother and she was half black. This meant that he, Jameson Lee Hartford, had African blood in his family's ancestry; he was part African! Imagine that! Jameson was dumbfounded as he told Delilah about his amazing find. His family must have been embarrassed of the patriarch and tried to hide the facts, but not quite mortified enough to completely destroy them. His great-great grandfather did not seem to be ashamed and must have lived with the woman as his wife. Too bad he would never be able to find out her name or the whole truth about his lineage, as all concerned had passed and all records were lost forever.

Delilah said, "That explains a lot about you doesn't it? You're more like me than you thought."

He smiled at her and said, "I'm proud to be even remotely related to you. Maybe your mother will like me now."

She smiled and said, "Hmmm, you never know."

He grabbed her and flipped her over unto the bed. They kissed passionately, then made beautiful love to one another. A love they had not experienced in some time. He forgot how soft and sweet his woman was; she forgot how strong and masculine her man could be.

He softly ran his hands over her body as she kissed him tenderly. They reveled in the moment thrusting their bodies in the rhythm of love, gyrating and moaning as they stimulated  each other further and further until their passion could no longer contain itself and they both let love burst inside as they cried in pleasure. Out of breath, they laid on top of one another still wanting the moment to last a little longer. Jameson told her how much he loved her; she smiled and pulled him closer.

They held each other for some time enjoying it to the fullest until Delilah rose and pulled a cigar out of the drawer. She struck a match, lit the cigar and took a long puff. She inhaled it deeply and blew the smoke toward Jameson. She climbed back into bed and snuggled up next to him, took another puff, inhaled and slowly expelled the smoke, asking him if he would like to share her cigar. He did. They took turns enjoying the tobacco and when it was done, they curled up in each other's arms and went to sleep.

The horses whinnied in the barn at a figure trying to open a door to a now blocked passageway. No one heard the disturbed animals and the mysterious person finally slithered off, disappointed at their failure to gain access to the great house. They would try again tomorrow, but as the figure tried to leave they were forced back into the barn by a group of unexpected visitors.

The calm of the evening was broken by the sound of horses and the whooping and hollering of its riders. All those who were asleep were suddenly alarmed and surprised as a bright light broke through the solid black night and lit up every window. Jameson, Delilah and the rest of the residents ran downstairs to the door and peered out into the yard.

A large burning cross was stuck in the ground. Its light was so bright that they all squinted and had difficulty believing the vision. When their eyes became accustomed to the glowing ember they noticed there was a sign placed next to it in the ground, reading:

White and Black don't mix. Get out!

Guns were fired into the air amidst whooping noises and veiled threats. Over and over they screamed and yelled obscenities as firearms were discharged, scaring the plantation occupants particularly the little children.

As Jameson went to get his gun, the horses and their riders were already galloping off into the darkness, like thieves in the night, no doubt to protect their identities. Jameson grabbed a bucket, filled it with water, raced into the yard and doused the burning timber. The residents were shook up and little Dawnalee and Ruby Rose both needed extra comforting from their mother and Nanny.

Jameson removed the cross from the ground and as he held it up a loud bang rang out of the darkness and a bullet came flying in, narrowly missing him but hitting the cross and knocking it from his hand.

Jameson fell to the ground for protection as Delilah cried out, "James!"

"I'm alright! Stay in there and get everyone away from door and inside the house, "he ordered.

"Who are you? Show yourself," Jameson demanded of the shooter.

"I'm here to take you in, Hartford; I have a wanted poster here that says you're a fugitive responsible for all those people you killed five years ago right here in Willow Hills. Frankly, I'm surprised you were stupid enough to return, well too bad for you but good for me. You have a price on your head and I am going to collect it."

"What are you a bounty hunter?"

"No matter, I'm now $1,000 dollars richer."

"You're too late, I already spoke to the sheriff about the matter and he released me on parole until the judge returns."

"I don't know anything about that, so I'm going to take you into town."

"You realize that poster was printed during the war and is only payable in Confederate money, which is now worthless, so you are still poor. Now you better get off my property, you're trespassing."

"What are you going to do, add me to the list and kill me too?"

"If I have to, I will."

"I can bring you in dead or alive, doesn't matter to me, I get my money either way. The choice is yours."

Delilah grabbed the rifle and watched as her husband tried to rise and move toward the house. Another shot rang out, narrowly missing the prostrate Jameson. Delilah raised the rifle to her shoulder, peered down the sight, aimed the barrel at the exact location of the burst of light from the exploding gun powder and pulled the trigger. A loud bang emanated from the gun and a moment later a scream came from the bushwhacker as he fell to the ground, quickly rose, jumped on his horse and beat a hasty retreat.

"I think I got him, James."

Jameson rose uneasily, worrying about a second shooter but the night was quiet again. He picked up the burnt cross and threw it to the side in an empty plot of land with no vegetation so as to avoid another blaze.

He walked back into the house shaking his head and wondered if they could change the minds of both the blacks and whites and have them work together.

He kissed Delilah and exclaimed, "You never cease to amaze me, that was quite a shot."

"I had a good teacher," she answered as she smiled back at him.

"Is everyone alright?"

"Yes we are all fine."

The children ran up to hug their father.

"James, do you think the people of Willow Hills did this?"

"I think we have to assume it was them."

"Why, we are trying to help them."

"Yeah, what is wrong with those people?" Nanny said.

"We will have to explain this to them in greater detail tomorrow and see where they stand," Delilah stated.

They all once again retired to their rooms and tried to go back to sleep, though they wondered if the plans they were about to execute were real or just fantasies. Their happiness was crushed and their sleep was uneasy.


The figure in the barn waited for all the candles and lanterns in the house to be extinguished, then crept onto a bale of hay and went to sleep for the night. They knew they would awaken when the sun came up and the roosters crowed and could be far away before anyone became the wiser. Perhaps tomorrow they would once again work on trying to gain entrance into the large plantation house.

# Chapter 5

## *Showdown*

The following day was one of planning and preparation. The first stop would be a trip to Charleston to purchase needed supplies, have money wired from Boston to the bank in Willow Hills, and order whatever else they were going to need for the businesses they were planning to start. School supplies, seeds for planting, materials and sewing supplies, saws for a lumber business, meat and potatoes, hardware items, glass for windows; there was so much! Did they forget anything? Oh and they would need a location for all these items, a large warehouse to store everything as they were starting to be delivered. For that they had to find suitable locations in Willow Hills. Jameson had to purchase a second wagon to accommodate all the materials they were going to haul back with them. He drove one and Delilah drove the other. Delivery men would provide the rest.

On the way they stopped at Black Woods so Delilah could see her mother again. This time they brought Dawnalee and eagerly introduced her to her grandmother for the first time.

"Oh my, she is so cute. Come give your Granma a big kiss."

Dawnalee was a little fearful but at the urging and pushing from her mother she was shoved in front of the older woman, who wasted no time in giving her a great big kiss that Dawnalee hurriedly wiped off.

"Dawnallee, don't do that. She is your grandma, my mother. She loves you just as I do. Now give her a kiss."

Dawnalee obeyed her mommy, puckered up and tried to give a quick peck to the cheek of the old woman. She was surprised as Leah grabbed her and held her lips against the child's for what seemed like an awful long time. She managed to pull away and again wiped the kiss from her lips to another reprimand from her mother.

Leah said, "Don't scold the poor child, she doesn't know me yet. Let her get used to her grandma. Isn't that right honey child?"

Dawnalee shook her head yes as she moved away from the woman.

"Child this here is your Aunt Ambrosia and Uncle Marcus."

They in turn took the child and hugged and kissed her much to Dawnalee's chagrin.

"Mama, have you changed your mind about coming to live with us at Serenity?"

"We talked about it and we will come provided we don't hafta have anything to do with that white man of yours. Honestly baby, why would you marry him? You can't trust a white man; he'll turn on you in a second and wind up hurtin' you."

"Mama, wait until I tell you what we found out about my husband last night."

"Did he cheat on you already, child?"

"No mama, Jameson discovered that he is part African. His great-great grandfather lived with a black woman, they had children and he is one of those descendants, so he is just like one of us."

"He don't got enough black in him to matter now, baby. He got no idea what's it like to grow up black. You just wait and see."

"Mama, James is a great man and he is not like that at all. Serenity is his house and if you are coming you will have to at least be civil to him."

"I'll be civil but I don't have to like or trust him."

They finally agreed to the move but wanted reassurances that they would not have too much contact with Jameson. Delilah hoped she could keep the peace.

"We'll do it for you baby, but not for the likes of him."

"Okay then, you can either come with us now or we can pick you up on the way back to Serenity tonight. What do you want to do?"

Leah looked at her children and, since they were all packed anyway, they decided to go along with them into town and see what they were really planning to do.

The promise of new housing would make the Black Woods shanty town disappear forever.

Jameson, in the meantime was gathering all the healthy able bodied men and women, who were eager for a chance to better themselves. They packaged up their belongings, piled them onto their rickety wagons and followed their hopes and dreams into the town where they were neither welcomed nor wanted. They marched forward to the unsuspecting town. The people of Willow Hills were not happy about this turn of events and were planning a retaliation of their own.

The townsfolk were massing in the street and another revolution was imminent. The blacks would be living and working in their town. They did not want this element sharing their living space. They worked hard to keep them out, forcing them to live in that shanty town, now they would be moving in and living right next door. This was not going to happen. A group was formed to discuss the matter which quickly turned into an angry mob. They came after Delilah and Jameson demanding they put a stop to their actions. Delilah decided this was the time to address the crowd. She found the highest point at the end of town, the gallows. She climbed the wooden structure and invited all to come and listen to her. It was ironic that a black woman would voluntarily stand where countless poor blacks were hung and now take charge and give orders to the people who once owned and abused them.

As she looked out on the crowd she knew this was not going to be easy. The people were amassed black on the left and white on the right, neither wanting to mix with the other. Delilah took a deep breath and began.

"My husband and I came back here to help my people, but that does not mean that I don't care about all the people. You are all welcome to join us, and work for us. We plan to rebuild the city, set up a school and shops and businesses. We will make this a great city and we can all share in it. We will use all available land and plant crops for food, as well as, cotton and tobacco. We can make and sell clothing, and roll cigars, both of which we can export to other cities and states. We will sell a lot of product and we will even pay you in United States Currency, not Confederate. The only thing you have to do is work alongside each other; we will all be equal here. Do you have a problem with that?"

She paused and waited for a second, then added, "And those people who came to my home last night and burned a holy cross on my lawn, you know who you are, you did not scare us. And the coward who tried to assassinate my husband also failed, he was not man enough to meet us face-to-face and talk like a civilized human being, he hid himself like the weakling he truly is."

She paused again looking intently at the somewhat astonished, yet puzzled assembly as one person in the crowd, Grayson Whitman, grabbed his bandaged arm and tried to hide the wound from peering eyes.

Delilah continued, "We are going to stay here; we will not be run off our property like the last time. If you have a problem with an interracial, mixed marriage, that is your problem; and that goes to both races, black and white. Jameson and I are married and we are very happy together and will stay together. Get over your bigotry; we are all human beings in the eyes of God. You have to forget your bias and work hand in hand, and give peace a chance. We can and will succeed and we will set a precedent for all other cities. What do you say? Can we do it?"

Most were dubious, but there were those who openly dissented.

"We won't be equal to you coloreds; you're not the same as us."

Delilah was furious but Jameson whispered in her ear, "Kill them with kindness. Don't treat them the way they treated you, you're better than that."

She smiled at him and rebutted, "If you think you are better than us; then by all means find your own jobs and with a little luck, you may succeed. Those who want to work hand in hand with my people, please join us, we would be happy to have you. There is a lot to be done and I will pay you out of my own pocket until our businesses start to show a profit. Again I ask you, are you ready to work and succeed?"

Mumblings were emanating from the crowd:

"What do you think we should do?"

"We need the money and the work."

"If we don't, she will give all the work to the coloreds and they will be better off than us."

"I'm going to join her. I want to be able to feed my family."

"I agree, we should give it a try."

They did not have to wait long for an answer. Most of the people were in need of employment and the almighty Yankee dollar changed a lot of minds. About eighty percent of the people accepted the terms and as the riot fell apart another ten percent decided to give it a try. Before it was over almost all the people wanted to be part of the recovery. But that was not the end of it. The black people now voiced their opposition.

"We thought you were going to help us. We don't want to work with a bunch of white people who once owned us and mistreated us. Let them suffer for a while like we did."

"Yeah, they should know what it is like to be poor and hungry."

"Let them be miserable for a while."

"We slaved for them, they owe us. They should pay us for all the work we did for them."

Delilah again had to display her arbitration skills.

"Listen to me, you have no education and no skills, you will always be at someone's mercy if you don't learn a trade and become responsible for yourselves. Use the gifts God gave you, don't squander them. Remember in the Bible the parable of the talents. How each man was given the gift of a talent: one man was given five talents, one man two talents and the last was given one talent. The Lord then left for a while and when he returned demanded a recounting of each man's life and how they had used the gifts he had given to them. The one with five doubled his to ten, the man with two also doubled his to four, but the man who was given one talent buried it and did not use it at all. The first two men were rewarded while the third who buried and wasted his talent was chastised and cast out into the night. The moral of this story is to use whatever talent the good Lord has given you, do not sit around and idle your time away. We all need to come together in this recovery or it will not succeed. Put your differences and hatred behind you for the good of everyone. There will be enough work for all of you. We will share in the responsibilities and the toil and then equally share in the profits. If you feel you can't do this then only those willing to work side by side with each other will be hired. I think we all need to consider the good that can come of this and, at least, give it a try. Show your children that there are no differences between us and that all people are indeed created equal in the eyes of God and can get along in this world."

The two sides looked suspiciously at each other and did not really want to work together but decided they had to do it. An uneasy peace was reached, at least for the moment and most agreed to her terms.

"To prove our new found friendship, let us tear down this appalling structure of unfair justice and start anew as neighbors."

The blacks cheered, the whites were silent, but the gallows was demolished that day. The work of rebuilding and reconstruction had begun in Willow Hills.

The sun was bearing down and it was another southern hot and humid day, yet through it all, Delilah barely broke a sweat. She was calm, cool and collected.

Sheriff Le Brute was amazed and thought he would never have lived to see this day. This would make his job easier. Taffeta Jones decided to add a few women of color to her establishment since the black men would soon have money burning a hole in their pockets and would need a place to spend it. Leah admired her daughter and was duly impressed, but not fully convinced. Michelle marveled at the determination of Delilah and vowed to add her to his trophy case. She was quite a woman, and having wealth only added to her allure for the evil Frenchman.

Marcus was looking at a young girl named, Victoria Whitman. He could not take his eyes off of her and she was enjoying all the attention from the handsome black man. He tried to get closer to her, inching his way through the crowd, until he was standing next to her. She was so lovely in her lavender dress and matching bonnet.

He got up the courage and said, "Hello, I'm Marcus, and who is this lovely creature I am talking to?"

She blushed and answered, "My name is Victoria."

"That is a beautiful name and you are a beautiful girl."

She blushed again as he asked her if he might court her.

"My father would never approve, I'm afraid."

"Do you always do everything your father tells you to?"

"Well, no not really," she giggled.

"Then how about meeting me?"

"Okay, come by my plantation tomorrow at dusk, but you better just wait outside for me by the tall oak tree."

"Okay, I'll be there."

"What is going on here?" interrupted her father, Grayson "Grady" Whitman, who was there to acquire his loan from the Hartford's, "I don't want you talking to this kind of boy, you understand me girl?"

"Yes, daddy."

"And you, you leave my daughter alone, understand?"

Marcus just looked at him but his eyes drifted to Victoria who mouthed the words *tomorrow* to him and smiled.

"Look at me when I talk to you, boy."

Marcus quickly changed his stance glared at Grady and retreated a step backward. Grady grabbed his daughters arm and hurriedly dragged her away. Marcus knew it was risky and probably not a good idea, but he also knew he would keep that date.


Doctor Pritchard called out from the side of his office, "Jameson, Delilah, come here for a moment, will you?"

They walked over and Jameson inquired, "Hello Doc, what do you need?"

"That was quite a speech there, Miss Delilah, I hope you succeed, I really do but I heard you say someone shot at Jameson last night at your plantation."

"Yes doctor, do you know something?"

"Well, Grady Whitman came to see me late last night with a gunshot wound to his left arm. He said his son accidently shot him while they were hunting for deer. I did not question him, simply took out the bullet, cleaned and bandaged his arm, but now…"

"James, he is the one who shot at you, let's confront him and have him arrested."

"Wait Lilah, this town is tense enough without having one of its own arrested. Let's forget about it for now."

"What? Why would you do that?"

"Well, once we loan him money, he will be in debt to us and I doubt he will try that again. He will owe us and we can win him over with kindness."

"I hope you're right, James, but I doubt a man like that can change. Thank you for telling us, doctor."

"You're very welcome and for what it's worth, I think you made the right decision."


People were already lined up all the way down the road to sign up for jobs and for school. Delilah started choosing people for various jobs, hired them and told them what she expected of them. Azure and Sienna were there in the front of the line as were all the people from Black Woods. The people from town also lined up but it seemed that the lines were delineated according to color. There were groups of blacks, then groups of whites, never quite mixing together. Perhaps that would come; at least that was the hope.

Delilah had found a suitable building to use as a school; the only problem was who could she get as a teacher? Madeline volunteered and was eagerly accepted. The children and probably most of the adults would shortly be going to school and learning how to read and write, for the first time in their lives. But all was not going to go so smoothly.

Abigail wanted to help, but Delilah had no use for her. At Jameson's urging, she was added to the teaching staff at the school, as so many people wanted to enroll and learn the basics that Madeline could not handle them all. Annabelle still had her nose in the sky and would not acquiesce to Delilah, who she still hated for taking Jameson away from her… and her sister.

Jameson took some of the applicants back to Serenity to start clearing the land, build decent housing and start a totally different life on the plantation. They would still work the fields but only for designated hours and they would be paid for their labor. Suitable housing would be built to accommodate the workers and their families. Each would have their own separate home with all the trimmings. It would be a completely novel experience, blacks and whites working side by side, equal work for equal pay, sharing in the bounty. Jameson was sure his experiment would be a resounding success.

With only four bedrooms in the plantation house, sleeping arrangements had to be adjusted. For the time being, Dawnalee and Ruby Rose slept on twin couches in the library. Madeline had her own room, Nanny had her own room, and the three newest boarders, Leah, Marcus and Ambrosia, had to share one room amongst them, much to their frustration and complaints. They had never been in such a large house and marveled at all the accoutrements. They wanted their fair share and demanded new clothes and everything that went along with their new stature in life.

Delilah saw to it that they got whatever they wanted and more. Jameson, on the other hand, it seemed, could do nothing right in their eyes. They complained about him incessantly and to whoever would listen.

There was new housing being built on the plantation for all the workers and their families and Jameson tried to get Delilah to persuade her mother and siblings to move into those spaces, but she wanted her mother close by, so that was not a viable solution. He hoped for a little peace, although neither Delilah nor Nanny could dissuade his mother-in-law and her siblings from tormenting him at every turn. He guessed it was payback for what his family had done to her in the past and tried to tolerate it. They took all their hatred and hostility that was bottled up for years and blamed it all on Jameson, even though he had nothing to do with any of it. He was now their whipping boy and they felt justified in their hatred of him. He avoided them as much as possible.

Materials kept coming and supplies of all kinds were warehoused in various buildings creating jobs of all kinds and new employees by the dozens. Delilah took charge of all these new businesses and the subsequent hiring and training, she was the boss and everyone knew it. It was taking up quite a lot of her time, making each day at work longer than the previous day. She missed her husband, children and mother more and more but could not shirk her duties. They would have to wait while she got all the businesses up and running.


Annabelle, jealous of Delilah, had concocted a plan to split her and Jameson up. She had a clandestine meeting with Michelle and offered to pay him a handsome stipend, if he could seduce Delilah and break up her and Jameson's supposed happy marriage.

"Why would you want such a thing, Mademoiselle?"

"I want him."

"You want your sister's former husband?"

"Yes. Jameson and I always loved each other. He would have married me but he had to marry my sister; a matter of honor or some such nonsense."

"What will your sister say?"

"I don't care. Will you do it or not?"

"I would have done it for free, but I will take your money."

"You can get her to have…relations with you, right?"

"My dear, the word is sex and yes I can, there is not a woman alive who can say no to Michelle Le Brute."

"A little conceited, aren't you?"

"Let me assure you, I am not a braggart. I have left a trail of broken hearts wherever I have visited. I can prove it to you if you would like to try your luck."

Annabelle was getting annoyed.

"Will you help me split up Jameson and his …wife?"

"Yes, I can and will do it, and not just for you, I want her too."

Annabelle looked surprised at the Frenchman but could care less about Delilah.

"Good, when can you start?"

"I will start when I feel the time is right."

"It better be soon, I can't wait forever."

"Don't worry; it will be soon, very soon."

"We have a deal then."

Michelle just smiled a wicked smile, shook his head in the affirmative and strode away. Annabelle left with a smirk on her face and vengeance in her heart. She had just made a deal with the devil.

# Chapter 6

## *Tryst*

Marcus was camouflaged in the woods overlooking Grayson "Grady" Whitman's plantation, "White Tranquility," and dare not proceed any further. He had come to meet Victoria Whitman at the appointed place and time as they had both agreed that day in town. They knew her father did not approve of an interracial relationship and would probably try to kill him if he found out. Still his yearning for her was strong and pushed him onward, clouding his better judgment.

Marcus was waiting what seemed like a long time when he heard a rustling in the brush next to him. He turned and there was his beloved, Victoria. She was dressed in a white blouse and dark blue skirt. Her auburn hair was pinned up on top of her head and her white complexion starkly contrasted with his dark skin. They hugged each other, knowing that they were toying with trouble; perhaps because it was taboo, made it all the more desirable.

"We shouldn't be doing this."

"I don't care if daddy finds out or not. I really like you and want to keep on seeing you."

"Yes, but you're not the one he will take his hatred out on."

They lay in the grass, holding each other as his mouth kissed her hand, arm, neck, mouth and then her chest. She breathed heavy, but offered no restraint, only encouragement. She unbuttoned her blouse and opened the lapels to allow him easily access to her breasts, which he eagerly pursued. They both wanted each other and did not care about protocol or proper behavior.

After a few minutes of heavy kissing and fondling, she stopped him and said, "We really shouldn't go any further, Marcus."

"I know but I want you so much."

"I have to go in before I'm missed and they come looking for me."

"Okay, okay, I understand, when can I see you again?"

"Tomorrow, come at the same time, around sundown."

"I'll be here, goodbye beautiful."

"Goodbye Marcus."

They kissed and then he watched as she disappeared back across the field and into the mansion. He got up to leave but was surprised by another rustling sound.

"Where do you think you're going, boy?"

It was Grady and his son, Grayson junior, who had a shotgun fixed on poor Marcus. There they were holding a black man at gunpoint for trifling with the only other young female in their life. What would they do with him? Grady was forced to join with Delilah and Jameson to acquire funds and be able to buy seeds, plant crops and hire workers. He was indebted to them and so had to be very careful with this matter of his daughter and Delilah's half-brother. He also saw this as a way to get even with them and perhaps hold the Hartford's at ransom for more money or perhaps to forgive his loan entirely. This had to be handled delicately, but there was no harm in putting a good fright into the lad. Scare him just a bit and get some retribution for all he had suffered because of the war.

"I warned you to stay away from my daughter, didn't I?"

"Answer him, you piece of trash you."

Trembling, Marcus answered, "Yes sir, you did."

"Then what in heaven's name are you doing here? Do you have a death wish?"

'No sir, I just… I just wanted to see Victoria again."

"That is never going to happen again, do you understand me, boy? You and my daughter are not going to be together, ever."

"Let's kill him dad. Right here, right now. We can bury him and no one will know the difference."

"No, please, my sister and mother know I'm here. They'll tell Delilah and Jameson."

"He's right. If those Hartford's found out I did anything to him, they would put us in jail and have us hanged."

They'd have to prove it first."

"Son, I borrowed a lot of money from those Hartford's and if they called those loans in, we'd be ruined. No we can't risk it."

"I wish this was like the old times when no one cared what you did to a colored."

"It isn't son, so we have to change with the times."

"So what do we do with him?"

"We let him go, with a warning."

"Can't we teach him a little lesson, like a good beating?"

Grady laughed, "I guess that can't hurt; at least not us."

Both men laughed and prepared to give the love struck Marcus a thrashing, just to teach him a lesson. Marcus was no weakling and as Grayson the younger came at him, he instinctively defended himself. The two men traded punches much to the humiliation of the elder Grady, who kept pointing the shotgun and threatening to shoot.

"Get away from him, son so I can get a clear shot at him."

Marcus kept the younger Grayson between him and the elder Grady to prevent any possible clear shot, but he knew he had to get away or he would be killed and they would claim self-defense. He landed a haymaker on Grayson sending him falling onto his father as the firearm accidently went off with a loud bang. Marcus watched in disbelief as Grayson the younger fell down on the ground with a large hole in his stomach and blood covering his body.

"My boy, my boy, what have I done, what have I done?"

Marcus turned and ran away as quickly as he could, back to his horse and galloped off to the security of his home.

He could hear Grayson in the distance wailing and then screaming. Marcus realized he could not tell anyone of this encounter as his mother and sister did not approve of interracial couples and hated Jameson. He himself had criticized their marriage and now here he was doing the same thing. His family would not approve so he kept everything to himself, hoping to simply forget the whole matter.


The next day was a beautiful southern day with bright sunshine and a warm breeze. Marcus could think of nothing else but the previous day and especially the lovely Veronica. He tried his best to forget her, but that face, oh that face, it just kept lingering in his mind. When evening rolled around, he could contain his lust for her no longer and decided to meet her as agreed the day before. He knew he shouldn't but he could not control his hunger to see her again.

He rode his horse to the White Tranquility plantation and carefully surveyed the horizon. The coast seemed clear so he ventured a little closer, and a little closer, until he spied Veronica waiting by the tree, their tree, where he met her just yesterday. He approached and still could see no one but her; perhaps he was blinded by love. He dismounted his horse, tied it to a tree and approached his heart's desire.

Veronica turned around and said, "Oh there you are, I was afraid you were not coming."

"I had to come to see you again and to tell you what happened yesterday."

As he was speaking, her father, Grady Whitman and Mordechai Le Brute, the sheriff emerged from behind another large tree.

"Put your hands up, you are under arrest."

"Under arrest, for what?"

"For the murder of young Grayson Whitman."

"What, I didn't murder him."

"Shut up you lying dog. If this were the old times I would hang you right here and now," said Grady.

"We'll have none of that, he goes to jail and has a fair trial, like anyone else."

"But, I didn't do anything. Mister Whitman shot his own son, honest."

"Shut up you piece of filth," Grady said as he backhanded a slap to Marcus's face.

""Stop that, Grady, or I'll arrest you too. Now come along peacefully son, don't make me tie you up."

"I didn't do it. Veronica, you have to believe me."

Veronica looked at Marcus and cried, "How could you do this terrible thing? I don't ever want to see you again."

She ran off into the house crying as the sheriff and Grady took Marcus into town and placed him in one of the cells.

News travels fast in a small town and soon Sienna came running into Delilah's office screaming, "Missus Hartford, Missus Hartford, they got your brother locked up in the sheriff's office. They chargin' him with murder."

"What?" the surprised Delilah remarked as she dropped her quill tip pen into the inkwell, grabbed her purse and made her way over to Le Brute's office.

She burst through the door and demanded, "What is going on here? Do you have my brother in jail? Is he charged with murder?"

"Yes, Missus Hartford, he apparently murdered young Grayson Whitman. He'll have to stand trial."

"That is preposterous sheriff, who brought these charges?"

Mordechai pointed to Grady and said, "Mister Whitman there."

"That's right, you're brother came to see my daughter, Victoria, yesterday and when me and my son told him to leave, he started a fight and shot my son with this here shotgun."

"Where did he get a shotgun?"

"It's mine ma'am. He took it from me and shot my son dead."

"I want to speak to my brother sheriff."

"Of course, Missus Harford, right this way."

Mordechai led Delilah into the jail area and let her into Marcus's cell.

Marcus was so glad to see his sister and told her the whole sordid tale. After a few minutes, Delilah emerged from the meeting and had a few questions of her own for Grady.

"Mister Whitman, you say my brother took your shotgun and killed your son, is that right?"

"Yes."

"Then what happened?"

"He dropped the gun and got on his horse and rode away."

"How many shots were fired?"

"Only one."

"So there was one shot left in the gun?'

"Yes ma'am."

"Why didn't he shoot you also?"

"I don't know, ma'am."

"Then why didn't you pick up the gun and fire it at him? Why would you let him escape?"

"I, uh, he, I was in shock, yes that's it, I was in shock."

"Sheriff, if a man is going to commit such a heinous crime, why would he only shoot one man and leave another eye witness there to identify him with a loaded gun at his disposal? And why would my brother come back again the next night if he was a murderer?"

"It is kind of suspicious. What do you say to that, Grady?"

"It's her brother, what do you expect her to say. Plus she's colored; she ain't gonna side with us whites. She's gonna side with her own kind."

"You didn't want my brother kissing and touching your daughter, did you?"

"No, why would I? He's not good enough for her."

"You mean he's not white enough for her, don't you?"

"Look, my son and I only wanted to teach him a lesson, you know rough him up so he wouldn't come back."

"You didn't think he would fight back, did you?"

"Well no, in the old days, a colored man would never raise his hand to a white man."

"So he fought back, got the better of your son and you had the gun and tried to shoot him."

"No, he, he came at me and, and, no wait my son was winning and…"

"You told Grayson to get away from him so you could shoot him."

"I, I had to defend myself and my son."

"Why would my brother think you were going to shoot him and then just leave you with a loaded gun so you could do just that, especially after he supposedly shot your son as you surmise? You shot your own son, didn't you, didn't you?"

Grady broke down in tears as Veronica was aghast at what she heard.

"It was a mistake. He fell on me and the gun went off, I didn't mean to do it. I'm sorry my son, I'm sorry."

"You tried to frame an innocent man? Oh daddy, how could you?"

Delilah demanded her brother be released immediately. Mordechai agreed and Marcus was a free man once again.

As he left, he walked by Veronica and said, "You didn't believe me. I told you I was innocent and you didn't believe me. You would rather believe the worst about me than the truth, why?"

She did not answer only hung her head in shame.

Delilah added, "Mister Whitman, don't think I haven't noticed that wound on your arm, if I could prove you were the one who tried to shoot my husband that night at our home I'd have you stand trial for attempted murder. I have no doubt it was you and believe me you won't cross me or my family again."

Grady was shocked but did not offer a rebuttal as Delilah and Marcus walked out the door into the street.

Marcus pleaded, "Delilah, please don't tell mama or Ambrosia about this, they wouldn't understand."

"You ridiculed James and I about our love, do you now regret your actions?"

"Yes, I'm sorry, if you're happy, I guess that's all that matters."


Delilah called in Grady Whitman's loan. He could not pay it and was forced to lease his plantation and all the surrounding property back to her. He begged for forgiveness, but Delilah could not forgive his lies and bigotry and wanted nothing more to do with him. He, his wife and daughter were now forced to work for her and she made him pay for his actions by requiring him to do menial labor and take orders from people he once considered below his stature. He dutifully obeyed for the sake of his loved ones, but deep inside, his blood boiled and he vowed revenge, even going so far as to try to convince the sheriff to enforce a law known as the "Black Codes." The sheriff refused so Grady tried to incite the other citizens of Willow Hills to follow him, but to no avail. People were making money and succeeding and did not want to upset the status quo.

Supplies were rolling into town and businesses were being started. School began to hold classes and all the children, both black and white attended together, sitting and learning right next to each other, proving racism had to be taught, it was not inherent.

There already was a sign at the entrance to Willow Hills dedicating the renewal and renovation of the town to Martha Barrington, but Delilah was extra proud to hang the sign at the dedication of the school: "Martha Barrington Memorial School." It made her feel fulfilled and insured that her mentor's name would forever be immortalized, and never forgotten.

Delilah was spending a lot of time opening and running the various new enterprises. Business was blossoming and she had the responsibility to instruct people on how the various businesses operated and teach them all the ins and outs. Women, who could sew, were making clothes. Women, who could cook, were canning. Others were running the shops, filling shelves and dealing with customers. People were coming in from neighboring areas because Willow Hills had such a wide variety of items to buy and eat. Delilah realized this was a monumental task and would require her to spend long hours in town each day. She acquired her own coach to enable her to travel back and forth between Serenity and her office in Willow Hills.

One day a white stranger complained that one of the cashiers, who happened to be black, gave her the wrong change and was trying to cheat her and demanded to see the manager. She was totally surprised to see Delilah come over and intervene.

"You are the manager?"

"I'm the owner. What can I do for you?"

"This woman tried to cheat me by giving me the wrong change."

"No I didn't, Miss Delilah. She gave me this here dollar bill and bought seventy five cents worth of goods, so I was giving her twenty five cents change."

"That's a lie! She added wrong and owes me more money."

Delilah looked inside her bag, dumped the contents onto the counter, quickly tallied up the items and said, "Madam, you are correct, let me see that change. Yes she mischarged you; you purchased eighty five cents worth of goods and are only entitled to fifteen cents change."

"Miss Delilah, she didn't buy that item, I don't know how it got in the bag."

The woman said, "I don't know where that item came from, honest."

"Madam, my cashiers know how to add, subtract, multiply and divide; they are not some ignorant, poorly educated colored girls and don't you ever treat them that way again; and don't try to steal from us again, or your business will no longer be welcome here. Now apologize to my employee."

The woman hesitated for a moment then apologized and quickly left the store.

"You have to watch everything, dear, some people are dishonest."

"I will, sorry Miss Delilah."

Delilah was now a force to be reckoned with; she was wealthy and powerful and people were beginning to not only respect her but fear her as well. That is everyone except, Michelle Le Brute, who admired her and wanted to harness that power for himself and would stop at nothing to achieve that end.

Jameson, on the other hand was fulfilling his dream of running a plantation with paid workers, proving it could be done and a handsome profit was there to be had. He still lamented that no one would let him prove that this would have worked prior to the war. He missed his wife a lot and whenever he could he tried to persuade her to forego her responsibilities and remain at Serenity. Delilah kept telling him to come into town and visit her, bring the children and oh yes, her mother too. Jameson promised he would try but her mother did not care for the rigors of travelling and preferred instead the comfort of Serenity.

One sunny afternoon as the two children were playing outside, with a ball fashioned of tightly wrapped rags, running all over the yard swatting it with wooden sticks, the object was hit a little too hard by Ruby Rose and flew over Dawnalee's head and landed in the woods. The child ran after it but stopped short of entering the forbidden area, just looking, hoping to spy the ball and quickly retrieve it.

"Don't go in there, Dawnalee," yelled Ruby Rose. "We'll get in trouble."

"I'm just going to get the ball," replied Dawnalee, "Don't say anything."

"No, Dawnalee, no."

'Shh, be quiet, I'll be back real fast."

As the child crept closer, she thought she could just make out the figure of a person dressed in a dirty white sack cloth peering out of the woods. She looked closer and could swear a pair of eyes were glaring at her. She froze in her tracks as she thought she heard a voice saying, *"Don't come in here child, go home, now."* The ball suddenly flew out of the darkness and landed all the way over by Ruby Rose. Dawnalee screamed and ran to tell Nanny, who immediately ordered Ambrosia to investigate. Nothing was there and no one was discovered. The children were reprimanded and told, yet again, not to go near the woods. Jameson would be told when he arrived home, but upon further investigation, nothing was found. Dawnalee stuck to her story and could not be convinced it was all in her imagination.

There was another impending problem, however; some people were becoming sick with a mysterious strain of an unknown virus. It was the same strain that had taken the life of Martha Barrington back in Boston and Jameson, Delilah, and Doctor Pritchard were all very concerned and monitoring the progress of the disease. Right now only a few were contracting it but if it spread and became an epidemic, panic would surely ensue. Doc decided to try to locate an anti-virus vaccine and purchase any serum that was immediately available to combat the impending situation.

# Chapter 7

## *Northerners*

It seemed like it would be just another day in Willow Hills, when two strangers arrived looking totally out of place and confused. The man and woman wandered around town as if casing the place for a robbery when the woman, in utter disgust, and at wits end began to ask for information. Some people just looked at them and walked away sensing trouble, while others laughed at their peculiar pronunciation. Finally, someone stopped and listened to their question, then pointed them in the direction of Delilah Hartford's building. They looked at each other and hurried across the dirty brown road in the route they had been shown.

Delilah was working, as usual, in her office when the woman and man threw open the door and demanded to know if she was Delilah Hartford. The dialect in the voice told Delilah they were from New England.

The man was dressed in a suit and tie with polished black shoes. His hair was slicked back and he held himself as if he were someone of importance.

The woman wore a long lace and silk dress with a small hat which had a thin veil that partially covered her eyes. She also stood tall.

Delilah eyed them up, carefully, noting that she had seen this woman somewhere before as she replied, "I am Delilah Hartford and who are you?"

"You don't recognize the woman whose life you destroyed?"

"You look familiar, but I can't place you."

"Well allow me to jog your memory. My name is Prudence Porter."

The name gave Delilah the shivers as she remembered the woman who tried to seduce her husband and when he refused she had him fired from his job. This was also the daughter of the banker Delilah had run out of business in her attempt at repayment for their cruelty.

"And this is my brother, Devlin."

"What can I do for you?" Delilah said very matter-of-factly.

Prudence said, "Is that all you can say to me? You ruined my life. You caused my father's bank to fail. You took everything from me. I'm poor."

"Why should that matter to me? You didn't care about me or my husband when you got him fired from his position and left us practically penniless. You were a rich spoiled brat; now you are a poor nobody."

"A nobody! I'll have you know I can trace my family roots back all the way to my ancestors who came over on the Mayflower. You are the nobody."

"Well I can trace my family roots all the way back to an unnamed slave ship, where my ancestors were kidnapped from their homeland and forced into slavery in an unknown land by your kind of people, who forced them to work from sun up until night, fed them scraps of food, gave them run down shacks to live in, whipped and tortured them, bought and sold them like animals and generally had little regard for either man, woman or child. So again, tell me why should I care?"

Nothing mattered to Prudence but her state of affairs as she fired back, "When you caused my daddy's bank to fail, we lost everything. My father committed suicide and my mother had a nervous breakdown. My brother and I were left to pick up the pieces, so you little piece of trash, how you dare talk to me like that."

Delilah felt a twinge of sadness but could not back down now.

"I'll talk to you any way I please and if you don't like it, you can leave my office. In fact, do that, get out, now!"

"Why you little…"

Prudence could no longer control her anger and charged Delilah grabbing her and forcing her to the ground. The two women wrestled on the floor, slapping at each other and ripping at their clothes. Prudence tried to pull Delilah's hair but it was too short for her to grab, however that was not the case for Prudence. Delilah managed to grab a large amount of it and pulled. It came loose and fell to the ground. It appeared Prudence was wearing a wig and had very little of her own hair. Prudence was aghast and humiliated by this turn of events and tried to get up and escape the fracas. Delilah was much stronger than Prudence and ultimately triumphed getting the upper hand and sitting on top of her repeatedly hitting her and yelling at her. Devlin grabbed and pulled Delilah off his sister and held her as Prudence got up and attempted revenge. The noise drew a crowd and within seconds the sheriff had arrived on the scene, ending the melee.

'What is going on here," he demanded.

Prudence grabbed for her wig and hastily placed it back on top of her head. It made her look quite comical as she struggled to position it correctly. She turned to her brother and told him to come along, they were leaving.

"Not so fast," said the sheriff, "You alright, Missus Hartford?"

"Yes I'm fine."

Delilah did not have a scratch on her and merely had to readjust her clothing to appear as if nothing had happened to her.

"Do you want to press charges?"

Delilah thought for a moment, feeling bad for Prudence's losses and in a moment of weakness said, "No, as long as they leave town and don't come back."

The sheriff looked at Prudence and Devlin who nodded yes; they would leave, and couldn't wait to do so.

They were ushered out of the building and sauntered away, but Prudence mumbled to her brother, "I'm going to get even with her and that husband of hers if it's the last thing I do."

They waited for a coach to take them back to the railway station in Charleston, plotting all along as to what would be the worst thing they could do to hurt Mr. and Mrs. Hartford the most. The answer came quite unexpectedly.

Jameson was in town with Nanny, Dawnalee and her new sister, Ruby Rose. Dawnalee wanted to see where mommy worked so they all traveled to Willow Hills. The children were excited and Jameson wondered what all the clamor was at his wife's office. He rushed in to find Delilah back at her desk working on paperwork; keeping track of sales and orders, salaries, profits and more profits. She was succeeding beyond her wildest imagination.

"Delilah, what happened?"

"Nothing, James, I'm alright. I just had a visit from Prudence and her brother."

"Prudence, oh no, see I wish you hadn't gotten revenge on her and her father."

"I know, I feel a little bad, but what's done is done. I can't undo it. She told me her father killed himself and her mother is sick."

"She didn't come all the way here to just tell you that. What else did they want?"

"I don't know, we never got to that. We had a shouting match and the next thing I know we're on the floor fighting."

"Fighting, on the floor, are you hurt?"

"No honey, I'm fine. Don't worry so; I can take care of myself. How are my mother and my siblings treating you?"

"Don't ask! They still don't like me and continually give me a hard time."

"I'll talk to them again, my love, they'll change, you'll see. They just need time, that's all."

Jameson only shook his head and exclaimed, "I hope so."

At that moment Dawnalee, Nanny, and Ruby Rose entered."

"Hi mommy," Dawnalee screamed as she ran to Delilah's open arms.

"Hi baby, how is my little dear today?"

"I'm fine. We came to see you."

"Hello Ruby Rose, how are you darling?" Delilah said hugging the child, "And Nanny, nice to see you, nice to see all of you."

"We want to see what you do, mommy," Dawnalee said.

"It won't be very interesting to you honey, but here I'll show you."

Delilah took them around the building and into the back room and tried to explain everything, but she was right, the children soon grew bored. Everyone was hungry so the whole family spent the rest of the morning enjoying their peaceful moments together at the only eatery in town. Nanny was not impressed with the food quality and to be honest, she was a much better cook.

Out in the street, behind a pole and just out of sight, Prudence was watching and hatched a plan.

"Devlin, do you see Hartford's daughter there. I just thought of the best way to hurt them. They took everything from me, so I will take the child from them. Then they will feel the heartache and loss that I have felt."

"Pru, that is a severe crime you're thinking of committing. If you get caught, they will hang you for that."

"I know, but I don't plan on being caught. Are you with me brother?"

"Do I have a choice? Of course I will help you; how do you plan on pulling this off?"

"We have to wait until the child is alone, we grab her and…"

"Where do you plan on taking her?"

"I guess back to Boston, where else? I don't want to stay in this God forsaken part of the country."

"They'll be looking for us and her in Boston."

"Well then we'll just sell her to someone or dump her someplace and let her fend for herself."

"You couldn't be that cruel, could you, sis?"

"I hate both of them so much; I don't care what happens to them or their child. Besides, it will hurt them forever if they can never find out what happened to their precious little girl."

Devlin shuddered to think his sister was capable of such an act, but since he was also destitute because of the Hartford's, he acquiesced to her wishes. The two malevolent siblings watched from a distance until the children, Jameson, and Nanny emerged from the building and got onto their wagon for the ride home. Jameson stopped at the bank to be sure the funds were still coming in and all the profits from their various enterprises were being deposited. Nanny never left the wagon, so Prudence could not make her move.

Prudence told Devlin to see if he could rent a carriage so they could follow Jameson to his plantation and carry out their evil plan.

Jameson emerged from the bank, boarded the carriage and started for home. Devlin arrived with his coach moments later and he and Prudence followed the Hartford wagon at a safe unobserved distance.

Soon after they left, a small regiment of Northern soldiers marched into town and stopped in front of Taffeta Jones Gentleman's Emporium, no doubt they had been there before, many times. They noted how the little town had grown and prospered.

The lieutenant in charge of the troop remarked, "We will have to see what all this is about and get our fair share; won't we men?"

He told his charges to go and enjoy themselves, they eagerly obeyed. He strode over to the sheriff's office to inquire of the changes.

Lieutenant Wellington wore his blue uniform proudly. He sported a handlebar mustache and the lines on his face displayed his battle weariness. He was an imposing figure, hardened by too much bloodshed and death.

"So sheriff, what has happened here since my last visit?"

"Oh no, not you again."

"Not happy to see me?" He laughed, "I don't really care, the question stands as posed."

Mordechai had no choice but to respond, "A couple of decent folks returned from the north and decided to invest in the town."

"Seems they did a good job; who is in charge?"

"Look lieutenant, this town is thriving and it is all due to them. I don't want to see them leave. I don't want any trouble."

"And you won't have any trouble as long as they are accommodating. You want peace don't you?"

"We are already a peaceful town and don't need your help."

"I'll be the judge of who needs my help, and as for peace, well that can be changed in a second, if you know what I mean? Now who is in charge of this… renaissance?"

Mordechai said he would take the lieutenant to see the person in charge and walked him over to Delilah's office. She was hard at work behind her desk, as usual, when they entered.

"Missus Hartford, this is lieutenant…"

"A lady in charge, and a lady of color, well good for you; I see the war was not waged in vain. You have elevated yourself admirably, I commend you, now, allow me to introduce myself, ma'am. I am Lieutenant Wellington. You are in charge, I am told?"

"Yes, lieutenant, I am Delilah Hartford and I am in charge of some of the businesses in town. What can I do for you?"

"Well ma'am, you know these southern towns can be quite lawless since the end of the war and my men and I have been charged by the United States government with providing much needed protection throughout these unruly towns. We travel between communities and keep the peace, safeguarding you against carpetbaggers, scalawags and the like. Danger is everywhere these days, ma'am."

"This town is quite law abiding, I assure you, lieutenant, and sheriff Le Brute is doing an excellent job, so we won't be needing your help."

"I don't think you quite understand me, ma'am. We offer our protection and guarantee you and your businesses the security you require, but there is a fee for that."

"Doesn't the government pay you, lieutenant?"

"Not nearly enough. We, unfortunately, have to charge business owners, such as yourself, for our services, or… unfortunate things could happen."

"Are you trying to extort money from me?"

"Extortion is such a dirty word. I prefer to call it protection."

Delilah turned to the sheriff and asked him, "Do you condone such actions, sheriff?"

"No I do not and I think you should go lieutenant and take your men with you."

"I will go, just as soon as I am paid for my services. I hate to think what would happen to you if the sheriff here decided to enforce the "Black Codes" that were passed by so many of these southern states."

Delilah looks perplexed and asked sheriff LeBrute, "What is the lieutenant talking about?"

"Missus Hartford, they are laws enacted to limit the rights of the newly freed blacks. I assure you I have no intentions of enforcing those laws here in Willow Hills."

"Ah, but suppose he changes his mind or is forced by the state to implement those laws, what would happen to you and all your businesses? You don't want something bad to happen now do you?" inquired Lieutenant Wellington.

"Are you threatening me?"

"Again, threat is such a dirty word; let's call it a promise instead."

"What would the government think of your actions, lieutenant?"

"The government will never find out; my men and I will see to that. Now if you'll just give me say fifty dollars. We'll be on our way, until the next time."

"How is that providing protection?"

"It's protection… from us."

"I thought you were supposed to be the good guys."

"We can be…the choice is yours; good is in the eye of the beholder, now how about that money, ma'am?"

Mordechai pulled his gun and told the lieutenant to leave.

The lieutenant laughed and said, "Do you really think you can stop me and my men? Why must it always be the hard way? Put away that gun before I order this entire town to be burned to the ground. I'm trying to be reasonable, but if you give me any more trouble, the price will go up to say seventy five dollars."

"Sheriff, I think we will just have to pay. I don't want to see all my hard work to go up in flames. Lieutenant, I don't have that kind of money here, I will have to go to the bank to acquire it."

"That will be fine. I'll be over at the tavern, uh, emporium, just don't try anything foolish."

He turned and walked out grinning at the sheriff, proud that he had won the altercation without firing a shot. The lieutenant walked over to Taffy's and entered the saloon.

Delilah and the sheriff walked nervously to the bank.

"Isn't there anything we can do?"

"I'm afraid not, Missus Hartford. I'm only one man and I am no match for them."

"Can we get some people together and arm them, maybe mount our own attack?"

While they were yet speaking, another group of soldiers rode up the street and into town, this time they were confederates, with all the soldiers sporting the double R patch proudly on the sleeves. It was Randall's Raiders. The captain, Rip Randall and his men still proudly wore the rebel gray uniform and had not yet conceded that the war was over. They spied the sheriff and rode right up to him.

"Sheriff, I am Captain Randall, we are trailing a group of soldiers who are threatening and extorting money from small towns all along the south; have you perchance seen them?"

Mordechai told the captain that the men he was searching for were indeed in town and were at this moment in the saloon down the street.

"Is that Lieutenant Wellington, sheriff?"

Mordechai nodded yes and told the captain of the extortion plot exacted on Delilah and the town.

The captain looked at Delilah and remarked, "They are extorting money from you?"

"Yes, captain, my husband and I are trying to rebuild the town and help all the people."

"What is your name?"

"Delilah Hartford, captain."

Rip Randall smiled and said, "Ah yes, I heard rumors in neighboring towns about some former southerners who had returned to their homeland and were trying to rebuild what the damn Yankees had destroyed. I just didn't realize that you were colored. Well that makes no never mind to me, trying to rebuild the south is a worthy cause and I support you in your effort, even if you are well, black. If the folks in this town don't care, why should I?"

He waited for a response but none was forthcoming as Delilah did not want to start another war.

"Very well then, let us handle it. We are still here to defend our beloved homeland from the filthy Yankees and after all, you are still southerners."

His military mind concocted a plot right there on the spot and ordered Delilah, "Stand out in front of Taffy's Emporium and call to the lieutenant, telling him you have his money. When he emerges, run away and find shelter, fast. Wouldn't want you to get hurt in the crossfire now would we?"

He smiled an evil smile that frightened Delilah and intimated that he would really like to see her perhaps be hit by a stray bullet. Delilah looked at Mordechai who just shrugged his shoulders and nodded. Captain Randall surveyed the area and instructed his men where to make their stand. He placed them all near the emporium, some on rooftops and others close to doorways, posts, alleys, anything that they could quickly hide behind once the gunfight started.

Delilah did as she was instructed but at first Lieutenant Wellington inside of Taffy's emporium responded, "Bring it inside, ma'am."

Delilah hesitated then answered, "I would not set foot inside that place; if you want it, come out and get it."

The lieutenant peered out from behind the swinging doors, surveyed the lone figure standing in the street, laughed and emerged onto the street. Delilah swiftly ran away. Out of the shadows emerged the daunting figure of Captain Randall and his men.

"Hello Wellington, we meet again, only this time we have the upper hand."

"Why hello, Randall, last time we bumped into each other, you and your men were retreating faster than General Lee."

"This time we are ready sir. You're under arrest for crimes against the south and the southern people."

"You have no authority here, be gone before I arrest you."

Randall responded, "I don't think you are in any position to give orders."

Lieutenant Wellington called to his men, who promptly put their clothes back on, downed one more drink and answered the threat. They all walked out into the street; seemingly one unafraid of the other and a staring contest began. It lasted only a brief moment as both sides went for their weapons and the thunderous sound of exploding gun powder filled the air. Shots were fired and answered over and over, until everyone's pistols were emptied. Smoke filled the dense humid air and no one could tell what had transpired. The fight was over in just a few seconds and there in the street lie the dead or wounded from both sides, but mostly blue uniforms. Wellington and what was left of his command ran for their horses, saddled up and rode away.

"You have not seen the last of us; we will meet again, Randall."

The captain and his men laughed heartily at what they all considered an idle threat.

The rebels were frantically reloading to give chase as Captain Randall ordered, "Find those traitors and finish them off."

The men jumped on their horses and gave chase. Having an enemy kept everyone alert and on their toes, besides they knew that if they killed Wellington another perhaps more sinister cavalry unit would be sent to replace him. It was a sport to Randall and his men, one they all enjoyed to the maximum. Know thy enemy was a mantra Rip Randall liked and lived by.

The Yankees that were still alive were silenced forever; there was no mercy and no feeling of regret for the enemy. Scores were settled and debts were paid, as the war, everyone thought had ended, still lived on in men's minds. Forever, indelible, memorable, it would never be forgotten.

Captain Randall ordered the doctor attend to his wounded men and then turned and addressed the curious crowd that had assembled, "I saved you and your lovely town from these evil Yankees and, unlike them, all I ask in return is food for me and my men; and maybe a drink or two and some lovely women."

Shots were heard in the distance and Randall remarked, "It is finished, the damn Yankees will bother you no more."

The people applauded him and he was quickly accommodated with meals, liquor and an enjoyable time at Taffy's.

"One other thing sheriff, I came here looking for a corporal of mine who was granted a leave of absence that was over a month ago. He has not returned. Has he been here?"

Mordechai Le Brute knew it was the soldier his half-brother, Michelle, had killed in a bar battle, but he feigned ignorance in the matter and the captain believed him.

"We will keep searching for him. I fear something has happened to him; maybe one of these Yankees killed him. Pity we didn't leave one of them alive so we could have interrogated him. Never you mind, we will find him."

Mordechai shuddered to think what would happen if they actually did find out.

Randall leaned in close to the sheriff and told him he wanted the "Black Code" laws enforced. That meant; remove this Hartford woman from her leadership role and place a white man or woman in charge before he returned again. Mordechai reluctantly agreed although he had no plans to act on the captains' order, but decided to just agree and avoid any more altercations.

The town was grateful to the southern soldiers, but Delilah remembered that these were the same men that she and Jameson had passed on the road the day they arrived in South Carolina. It was they who had tarred and feathered that poor black woman right in front of her daughter, Ruby Rose. She wanted to confront them but decided not to provoke an already volatile situation, besides she was not sure who the good guys were anymore or if they ever existed in the first place.

Delilah returned to her office and went back to work; there was still a lot to be done. In all this excitement, she had forgotten about Prudence and her brother; the same could not be said for them.

# Chapter 8

## *Best Laid Plans*

All seemed normal at Serenity as Jameson went about his work, Nanny tended to her chores and the two young girls played in the yard, unaware that they were being observed by a pair of evil eyes.

Prudence and Devlin boldly drove their coach past all the workers and their newly built homes, directly up to the side of the barn. As long as they did not look suspicious, everyone would think that they were just visitors. They stopped short of the house, turned the coach around, for a quick getaway and placed it just out of sight of the main house. Prudence and Devlin disembarked and walked slowly and carefully toward the unsuspecting children. No adults were in sight so they walked up to the two girls and pretended to be their friends.

"Hello children, how are you today?"

"We're fine. Who are you?"

"We're friends of your mommy and daddy. What are you doing?"

"Playing."

"Would you like to play a game with us?"

'We're not supposed to talk to strangers."

"We're not strangers honey; we know you're mommy and daddy. Your mommy works in an office in town and your daddy used to work in a bank in Boston. Now how would I know all that if I didn't know your parents?"

Both children just looked at each other and then shrugged that it must be alright as they seemed to know everything about their parents.

"So do you want to play a game with us?"

"Okay."

"Let's play hide and seek."

"Yes, we like to play that."

"Okay, you two run off and hide with my brother and I will cover my eyes and count to ten. Hurry now, go and hide. One, two…"

Prudence pretended to count as Devlin told one of the girls to go into the barn, while he led the other one to his coach. Whereupon, he grabbed her, gagged her and tied her up. He placed her under the seat of the carriage so no one would see her and motioned to Prudence.

"Ten, ready or not here I come," said the evil woman as she ran directly for her wagon. They smiled at each other and took off slowly down the road to attract as little attention as possible.

Nanny came out of the house and called for the children. She had seen the two adults and wondered who they were.

She called again and said, "Come here at once, children. Dawnalee, Ruby Rose, where are you?"

Obeying Nanny, a child came running out of the barn, it was Dawnalee. Prudence and her brother had inadvertently kidnapped the wrong child.

"Where is Ruby Rose?"

"We were playing hide and seek with mommy and daddy's friends."

"Where are they?"

"I don't know. I don't see them."

Nanny panicked and called, "Mista Jameson, Mista Jameson, come quick, I think someone took Ruby Rose."

Jameson raced out of the house. Nanny and Dawnalee explained what had happened. He surmised it was Prudence and her brother and realized they probably wanted Dawnalee and didn't know they had taken the wrong child. That did not matter as one child was just as important as another and he was going to save Ruby Rose. He saddled a horse and rode out to his workers inquiring of them what they had seen. He was told of the coach coming and leaving shortly afterward. They pointed in which direction the coach was headed and Jameson was off in a flash.

They did not have much of a head start so he figured he should catch up to them in a matter of minutes. Besides, he could see the freshly made tracks on the dirt road. He was having no problem tracking them and pushed his horse harder.

Prudence and Devlin were going along at a brisk pace, heading for Charleston and the train to Boston. The coach was bumping along on the uneven road, making it impossible to go any faster.

Ruby Rose was crying and trying desperately to untie the rope which bound her. She managed to free her hands and pulled off the gag. She crawled to the back of the wagon and thought about jumping off, but fear prevented her from completing the deed. Prudence noticed the child and told Devlin to stop the wagon. He obeyed. As the coach came to a halt, Ruby Rose jumped off, fell in the dirt, picked herself up and began to run. Devlin followed in close pursuit, gaining on the child with each step.

Ruby Rose sensing capture ran off the road and into the reeds and weeds, not losing a step. The tall grass kept hitting her in the face as she plunged forward with little regard for the small cuts the sharp plants were inflicting on her.

Devlin was not happy that he would have to go into the fields as it would ruin his suit and shoes, but he had little choice in the matter. He too was receiving cuts from the reeds and was getting angrier and angrier. He could see the little child but she seemed to always be just out of his reach.

Finally he was able to grab the collar on her shirt and pull her down, as she screamed, "Let me go, don't hurt me."

He placed his hand over her mouth to silence her and held her tight to prevent any further escapes. He turned to make his way back out of the field and onto the main road.

Prudence was pacing back and forth, waiting for her brother to complete his task, when she spied a horse in the distance, approaching fast. She supposed it was Jameson and panicked, yelling to her brother to hurry up.

Devlin emerged from the field, his face cut and his expensive suit torn in several locations. His captive tucked neatly under his arm, he ran back and jumped onto the wagon.

He threw the child at Prudence and told her, "Keep the little brat quiet."

He turned around to witness the approaching horseman. He pulled a derringer he had hidden in his coat and checked to be sure it was loaded. He only had two shots in the small pistol and had to make them count. He told Prudence it was no use and they would have to face their nemesis here and now, as they could not out run a horse with only one rider. He placed the gun against the child's head as Jameson approached.

"Stop right there, if you come any closer I will shoot the child."

Jameson halted, dismounted and tried to reason with the two kidnappers.

"Remember me, Jameson?" Prudence said. "Your wife ruined my family and now I will ruin yours unless you turn around and ride off."

"Prudence, did you forget you ruined my life first. You didn't feel any remorse for that, did you?"

"You deserved it for jilting me and marrying that… woman."

"Prudence, poor misguided Prudence, you and I were never a couple. I never promised you anything and besides that, you have taken the wrong child. That little girl is not mine; she is a friend of my daughters."

Jameson thought that if they knew the child was not his, they might let her go.

"What! That can't be. Devlin, you took the wrong child."

"How was I to know which one was his, you didn't know either."

Prudence thought for a moment; then added, "It doesn't make a difference; I'll still kill her."

"She is just a child, please let her go. It's me you want, take me instead."

Devlin and Prudence were confused. In their haste, they had taken the wrong child and now Jameson and Delilah would not feel the hurt they had hoped to inflict on them. Prudence told Devlin, "Forget the child; shoot Jameson, do it now!"

Devlin pointed the gun at Jameson and pulled the trigger as the intended target jumped into the brush to avoid his proposed fate.

"Did you get him? Did you get him?" Prudence yelled.

"I don't know," replied Devlin.

"Well go check."

Devlin jumped off the wagon and cautiously walked toward the spot where he last saw Jameson. He squinted into the reeds and tall grass hoping to see Jameson's figure, his shadow or at the very least, some blood, which would indicate that he was wounded; but he saw nothing.

Another group of horses were coming up the road and Prudence yelled to Devlin, "Who is that? We better get out of here."

Devlin ran back to the coach and they started to race toward Charleston, but they were no match for the approaching riders who seemed to come out of nowhere and overtake them.

Prudence looked at the mounted riders and panicked when she realized they were actually soldiers, in grey uniforms. It was Randall's Raiders.

They stopped the coach and Devlin asked them, "What do you want?"

Prudence echoed, "Yes, what do you want?"

Unfortunately, their strong New England accents and manner of dress revealed where they were from and instantly exposed them as the enemy.

"They're Yankees, sir!"

"Yes, I can tell that, sergeant."

The captain cross examined them: "Who are you? What are you doing here? Where are you going? Why do you have a black child with you?"

Ruby Rose recognized the men who had killed her mother, bit Prudence's hand, screamed and broke free of the evil woman's grip. She jumped off the wagon and started to run down the road. Jameson emerged from the grasses and scooped her up in his arms, trying to calm her down.

"Are you alright honey? Did they hurt you?"

She shook her head no, but she was still covered in drops of blood and her dress was torn from running through the sharp reeds in the field.

The captain yelled, "Who are you, sir?"

Jameson looked totally disheveled from his encounter with the tall grasses and was also cut and bleeding. He related his story to the captain in his best southern drawl, so they would know he was a southerner, born and bred. Ruby Rose was crying and begged Jameson to take her home. She was terrified of these men.

"Are you the guardian of that child, sir?"

"Yes, captain, I am."

"How did these people come to have her?"

"They took her, captain. I was coming to save her."

Prudence was outraged that her secret was now made public and her vendetta against Jameson was falling apart. She grabbed the gun from Devlin, aimed and fired at Jameson. The bullet came close to its intended target but ultimately landed inches from his horse, kicking up gravel and rocks. The captain's men quickly disarmed her and held her at bay. Devlin put his hands up in front of his face and begged for mercy.

"I'm a gentleman, not a fighter."

"Too bad for you," said one of the soldiers as he hit him squarely in the jaw, sending him down to the dirty road.

The captain motioned to Jameson, "You are free to go sir, and I suggest you leave right now."

"Thank you for your help, captain. Will you help me bring them back to town to face justice?"

"No need for that. We will dispense justice right here, right now."

Prudence pleaded, "Jameson, help us, don't leave us here."

Jameson tried to intervene, "Captain, I will see to it that they pay for their deeds."

"I suggest you leave right now, before I hold you in contempt of my court, assume you are obstructing justice and decide I have been too lenient with you. GO NOW!"

Ruby Rose pleaded, "Please daddy, take me home, I'm afraid."

Jameson looked at the little terrified child and wasted no time. He mounted his horse, holding the child tightly against his chest and turned to leave. He could not resist one more glance back as he heard Prudence screaming and witnessed the soldiers tearing off her clothes, preparing to partake in some unthinkable act. Others were building a fire and heating up what Jameson figured to be black tar. This was not going to be pretty. He wanted to do something to help, but there was nothing he could do about it and he wanted no part of it, or those soldiers; so he rode for home.

He heard blood curdling screams in the distance as he put as much mileage as he could between them and the poor little girl they were going to hurt. He felt no sympathy for them, only pity. Two northerners in the hands of southern vigilantes, there was no telling what would become of them. Nameless faces in a cruel world, lost forever. That's just the way things happened sometimes.

He took the child back to Serenity where she was attended to by Nanny, cleaned, bandaged and given some extra sugar cookies to make her forget that horrible experience. Children are resilient and in a short time she and Dawnalee were playing once again in the yard as if nothing had happened.


Delilah was hard at work in her office, oblivious to the fact that her daughter was almost kidnapped. It was late and her stomach was growling she realized she hadn't eaten since breakfast and was ravenous. The restaurant was her only option and so she departed the building for the short walk to the eatery. She locked the door to her office and began to stroll down the street, waving to townsfolk along the way.

A lone figure lay on a roof across the street carefully aiming his rifle at the unsuspecting traveler. Grayson "Grady" Whitman could not take the humiliation of working and having to take orders from a black woman any longer. His usual white attire was replaced with all black so he would blend in with his surroundings and become as invisible as one man could. He was poised to take out his antagonist and right the wrong he felt had been inflicted on him for far too long.

The street was crowded and he could not get a clean shot at her, so he laid in wait biding his time, after all she would have to leave the restaurant and walk back to her office at some point and he would be waiting. All he needed was one shot to end his agony and free him of his indebtedness, or so his deranged mind thought.

He waited and waited getting more and more impatient as the time wore on, and then suddenly there she was walking down the street. He braced the rifle against his shoulder and looked through the sight and down the barrel leading his victim. His finger was on the trigger and he squeezed it ever so slightly as Delilah strolled by totally unaware of the sniper. The sound of the exploding bullet made everyone in the street stop and look. The recoil of the blast made the rifle flitch and forced the bullet to hit the building pillar precisely as Delilah passed in front of it. She looked up to see the shooter on the roof and continued to hide in back of the large wooden pillar to obstruct any further attempts on her life. Grady panicked, realized his cover was compromised and stood up to flee the scene. In his haste, he lost his footing and slid down the steep grade of the roof and plummeted to the street below. Temporarily dazed he could not rise quickly enough until a crowd had surrounded him, including the sheriff, Michelle and Delilah herself.

Grady ranted, "I just wanted to teach her a lesson that you can't treat people like trash and make them work so hard and demoralize them both mentally and physically. We're human beings after all, aren't we? You all know what I mean, don't you?"

The town's folk were silent and just kept staring at him.

"You mean like you treated my people for so many years?" Delilah answered.

Grady had no answer to her accusation. How could he defend himself when he mistreated his workers in the same manner?

He suddenly realized what he had done all those years and broke down and cried.

"I'm, I'm sorry Missus Hartford, truly sorry. I was a fool. I wasn't thinking about it that way at all and I should have. I'm sorry. Do what you want to me I deserve it."

Grayson Whitman was arrested and carried to jail, he had broken his good leg in the fall and it would have to be set by the doctor. He would only be able to hobble around for the rest of his life needing a cane for balance.

He did repent and tried to make up for his past evil actions. Inadvertently, Grady Whitman had exposed a wound that was smoldering in the town. Because of him, more people realized the truth that all men are created equal and color does not matter. A new era began that day, as the story spread and blacks and whites seemed to be able to work together, in peace, the way God had intended all along.

# **Chapter 9**

# *Affairs*

Delilah was working long hours in town, neglecting Jameson and her child. She now owned almost all the businesses in Willow Hills, which took up all her time; she seldom ever went home, but spent the nights in town. The only way Jameson managed to see her more than on weekends was to visit her in town. She had taken to wearing a long skirt and blouse instead of a lacy dress, which she thought made her look more authoritative. She was smoking way too many cigars, causing her to cough and lowering her voice almost an octave. She had let her hair grow out, preferring a more natural coif. Jameson wasn't sure if it was her choice or she was responding to Michelle's aspirations. Delilah had definitely changed, immersing herself in her many outside interests and forgetting those who once held that important position in her life. People were referring to her as the man of the house which infuriated Jameson.

After work, one night, he decided to go into town to confront his ever absent wife. Besides, he noticed more of his people were getting sick. They had come down with sore throats, fevers and a bad hacking cough. While he was in town, he would speak with Doctor Pritchard on this matter and see if he had any luck locating medicine.

Michelle had tried on several occasions to seduce Delilah, but to no avail. She was not interested in him or anyone, just her many business interests. Unfortunately, he would not be dissuaded and chose this very night to try and cajole her and win the winsome dark skinned beauty as his own. He was determined to steal, at the very least, a kiss from her voluptuous lips. Besides, he did have that arrangement with Annabelle, which he accepted and viewed more as a challenge to his manhood than a monetary contract.

"Good evening, my Cherie amour, you look lovely tonight, as usual. There is something about a beautiful woman in a shirt that is irresistible, and those pearls, where did you ever acquire such a beautiful necklace?"

"Are you here again? I told you to leave me alone. Now please go."

Michelle approached her and placed his arm around her, "You know you want me my love, why fight it."

"I don't want you. I have a husband and I love him. Leave me alone."

Delilah took a large puff of her cigar, inhaled it and attempted to blow it in Michelle's face, but he opened his mouth and placed his lips squarely on hers, breathing her smoke directly into his lungs. She pushed him away as he expelled her smoke.

"See, we are meant to be together."

"Get out of here now, or I'll…"

"You'll what, my dear, scream? No one will hear you and even if they do, I'll deny it. Admit it Mon Cherie, you liked it, didn't you?"

Delilah nervously sucked on the cigar, inhaling puff after puff, expelling the smoke through her nostrils as she inhaled the next puff, wondering what to do.

"There is no use in fighting it, Cherie, I've got my mind set on you and what Michelle Le Brute wants, Michelle Le Brute gets."

It was at this moment that, Jameson entered the building and was surprised to see Michelle there. He looked at Delilah and then back at Michelle.

"James, what a nice surprise."

"I have been taking care of your wife for you, monsieur."

"That's not true, James, nothing happened between us, I swear."

"Then why do I have traces of her lipstick on my lips?"

Michelle picked up a piece of cloth from the counter and wiped his lips, holding it up to Jameson for inspection, and saying, "See I told you. It is true."

"No, it isn't. He forced himself on me, James. You have to believe that."

Jameson was infuriated and rushed at Michelle, who quickly pulled his sword out of its scabbard and pointed it directly at his quarry.

"Stop James, he'll kill you," Delilah screamed.

Jameson halted as Michelle taunted him further, "My blade is bigger and harder than you. Perhaps if you were more of a man, your wife would not be here with me."

Jameson retorted, "A real man wouldn't have to hide behind a blade."

"I am not hiding, certainly not from you, the lady of the house."

Suddenly, a shot rang out and both men turned toward Delilah, who was brandishing a gun, "Get out Le Brute before the next bullet goes through you."

"Alright, I will leave, but I had a most enjoyable time my love. We will do it again, no?"

The gunshot brought the townsfolk running to see what had happened. The sheriff pushed his way through the crowd to see his half-brother exiting the store, laughing under his breath. He was proud of all he accomplished; placing doubt into the mind of a jealous husband.

"Is everyone alright?" Mordechai asked.

"Only a severely bruised ego," laughed Michelle, "No bloodshed."

"Alright everyone, move along, nothing more to see here."

"Keep that brother of yours away from my wife, or I will kill him," Jameson demanded.

"I will speak to him," Mordechai said, "as long as everyone is alright."

"We are fine," said Delilah, "but if Michelle comes here again, I will shoot him and in a place that he will regret."

Mordechai was surprised and a little embarrassed. He shook his head and exited the office.

Delilah ran up to Jameson and kissed him, telling him that she loved him and only him; trying to reassure him that nothing had happened. He was humiliated in front of the woman he loved and the whole town and took out his frustration on her.

"I want you to come home now!"

"I can't yet, James, I have a lot of work to do."

"I don't care about the work or anything else, only you. You're changing and not for the better."

"James, try to understand, I have a lot of responsibility to all these people. They rely on me for their livelihood. I can't just leave."

"What about your responsibility to me and our child?"

"Oh James, you, Ruby and Dawnalee are fine. I'm sure Nanny is taking good care of all of you."

"You don't even know that Prudence and her brother tried to kidnap our child."

"What… tell me what happened? Is my baby alright?"

"Yes, she is fine. Prudence and her half-witted brother kidnapped Ruby Rose instead, but I saved her and Prudence, well let's just say her and her brother will not bother us ever again."

"What did you do to them?"

"It wasn't me, it was those southern soldiers."

"You mean Randall's Raiders?"

"Yes, but how did you know?"

Delilah related her story and Jameson got upset all over again.

"What else could go wrong, you need to be home with me. It was not a good idea coming back here."

"Don't be silly, we are making a difference, a big difference."

"What happens if that Frenchman comes back?

"That's what I have the gun for, my love."

"Delilah," he only called her by her full name when it was serious, "I want you to leave with me now! I mean it."

"I'll come in a little while, ok, I promise. I just have to finish up a few things. Give me an hour, sweetheart."

"I'll be waiting at Taffy's, having a drink. You have one hour."

Jameson stormed out, forgetting all about the doctor. Delilah knew she should have followed, but thought it was a bad case of male ego and he would get over it. *"I'll go later,"* she supposed. *"He's just acting like a jealous guy, that's all it is."*

Jameson sat at Taffy's having one drink and then another, and another, and still another, as the time past, one hour, two hours, three hours. He was complaining to poor Taffy the whole time, and she was getting sick of hearing the same story over and over. Her job was to listen to disgruntled husbands, and get them to spend their money on her saloon girls, alcohol and maybe a quiet affair, but Jameson was so in love that he was not interested in anyone else. She would not make any other profits off of him.

She finally said, "You've had enough Jameson, go home. Let your wife work if she needs to and just forget about tonight."

He stumbled out the door and walked in the direction of Delilah's office. The light was still on and he glanced in; there she was still hard at work, smoking another cigar. He thought to himself, *"I'm not gonna beg her anymore and look like a fool. The hell with her, I'm going home."*

He climbed onto his horse and started the journey to Serenity. He was so drunk he could hardly remain in the saddle and almost fell off a couple of times. Luckily for him, the horse seemed to know the way and trotted along without much direction. When he looked up, he was surprised to find himself home so fast, as he dismounted in front of the plantation.

He stumbled up the porch steps and opened the door, saying, "Honey, I'm home."

He fell into the waiting arms of Abigail, his former wife. He had inadvertently ridden his horse to Tall Oaks, not Serenity.

"Jameson, is that you? Why you are so drunk."

"I know. I'm sorry honey. Help me to bed will you?"

Abigail did not know what to do, but knew one thing; he was in no shape to get back on a horse and try to find Serenity. She led him up the stairs to her bedroom, so he could sleep it off.

He grabbed her, kissed her and said, "I missed you honey."

Abigail half wanted to put up a fight while the other half wanted her ex-husband back. The attraction was still there, it had never left, and as she tried to take off his boots, the two of them fell into her bed, kissing and caressing each other as if they were still a couple. Their fever grew and they gave into temptation, taking off each other's clothes and making love just like the old times, only better, because this time it was forbidden. He kept telling her he loved her and she kept believing it. As the excitement grew inside of them, they both consented and committed the act moaning with pleasure. It was something she hadn't felt in such a long time and ached to feel one more time. The heat of the moment engulfed them both and they writhed in ecstasy until the deed was climaxed. He was so drunk and tired; he rolled over and went right to sleep. She only reveled in the feeling, hoping it would last after tomorrow morning.


Annabelle was busy in town, asking Michelle why the seduction was taking so long.

"You had her all alone, what happened?"

"Her husband showed up. What could I do?"

"I don't want Jameson hurt, under any circumstances, you understand?"

"That is why it is taking longer, Cheri. If he were out of the picture, it would be easy."

"I thought you were supposed to be so irresistible, such a ladies man, at least that's what you told me."

"I will seduce her, don't you worry your pretty little head."

"You're not a real man. You can't even get a colored woman to fall for you."

Michelle slapped her across the face and said, "Shut up!"

"How dare you slap me!"

"Be quiet, you fool. I will succeed. No woman has ever refused Michelle Le Brute and this one shall be no exception."

"I hope not," Annabelle said as she walked away, "especially if you want that money, and don't you ever lay a hand on me again, do you hear me?"

"Annabelle, I believe you are the kind of woman that secretly enjoys a little slap now and then, Are you not?" he said with a wry smile.

Annabelle just stared at him, wondering what kind of person she had gone into business with and decided it would be best to just leave…and she did just that.

Unbeknownst to her, the man she was after was at that moment, in her house making love to her sister.

# Chapter 10

## *Morning After*

The sun crept from the window across the floor to the bed, and up the covers until it reached Jameson's eyes. He awoke and looked around. *"Where am I,"* he thought. He did not recognize his surroundings. A bigger shock came as he realized he was naked. His clothes were strewn about the floor. He rose and fell back into bed with a huge headache. It was coming back to him now; the fight with Delilah, the drinks at Taffy's, and….OH NO! Abigail! He was in Abigail's house and he… *"Oh no…I couldn't have…Could I?"* he thought.

He gently and slowly rose and reached for his clothes, getting dressed as fast as the hangover would let him. He crept down the stairs and there was Abigail in the kitchen.

"Oh Jameson, I see you're up. I made you some coffee, strong black coffee. Come here sit down and have some, it will make you feel better."

She was in a very good mood, kind of gliding across the floor as she moved, almost as if her feet were not touching the ground. She looked lovely in her nightgown and silk robe cinched loosely about her, allowing a gentleman a peek every now and then.

"Abby, I have to apologize for last night. I did not know what I was doing. I had a little too much to drink."

"You had more than a little too much. It reminded me of the time at that barbeque, a few too many years ago, when you were enjoying your mint juleps. Do you remember that? You thought you could ride that bull and I do believe you were really going to try it if…"

"Abby…I have to leave. I have to go home… to my wife."

She stopped what she was doing as the smile left her face and she came back to reality.

"Yes, I suppose you do. I guess I was hoping that, well never mind, at least have some coffee before you go."

"Yes thank you, I will."

As he was sipping the strong coffee, Annabelle, trotted down the stairs and was stopped in her tracks by what she saw.

"Jameyson, is that you? Here with us? In our little ole home? My…what a surprise."

"Annabelle, don't get any ideas, Jameson just stopped over for a visit and some coffee, that's all," said Abigail.

Jameson just winked at her, but Annabelle would not let it be. She noticed how disheveled he was and quickly put two and two together.

"You spent the night, didn't you?" she asked him. "Did you two make love?"

"Annabelle, stop that kind of talk right now," Abigail demanded.

"I should be going," Jameson said as he arose from the table and headed for the front door. "Thank you for your hospitality, Abby."

They both stared at each other and wondered if the other could keep the secret. Then he mounted his horse and rode away.

Annabelle approached Abigail and said, "He's gone, now tell me what really happened last night. I know he spent the night, I saw him leave town and he was drunk. You can tell me, I'm your sister."

Jameson approached Serenity in late morning and everyone was already at work, wondering what had happened to him. He made no excuses, just rode up to the house and went to his room to get cleaned up. He noticed his bed was rumpled and inquired of Nanny if Delilah came home last night, she had, but left early in the morning to go back to work. He had missed her. Nanny could see the hurt look on his face and worried that if something was not done soon, their marriage would dissolve. She decided that she would have a talk with Delilah as soon as she could. Nanny was also curious as to where Jameson was last night, and, in her usual brash manner, came right out and asked him. He hemmed and hawed and stuttered and never quite answered her. Nanny knew something was wrong. She also needed to tell him something else, but decided this was not the right time as it was too upsetting; she would wait until he cleaned himself up a bit.

Leah and Ambrosia also noticed Delilah's absence, and of course, blamed Jameson, saying they knew it wouldn't last. They were hoping to end what they considered a travesty.

"An African woman and a white man were not meant to be together. It is just wrong."

They did not miss an opportunity to make malicious, hurtful comments about him. Their remarks were especially cruel this morning perhaps because of his hangover or because he really missed his wife. He could do nothing right in their eyes and even Nanny could not change their minds or get them to stop. It seemed there was rampant racism on both sides with Jameson and Delilah stuck right in the middle.

They railed at the poor man and berated him unmercifully.

"Look at you comin' home at this hour and stumblin' around all drunk; and in front of my grandchild."

"You're just no good white trash."

"Don't know what my daughter saw in the likes of you."

"What a poor choice for a husband you are."

He was in no shape to argue, just absorbed their insults and meekly walked upstairs to try to refresh himself.

After this particularly nasty confrontation, little Dawnalee walked up to her grandmother and asked with a childhood innocence, "Nanna, why are you so mean to my daddy?"

Leah bent down to be close to the child and said, "I'm sorry to have to tell you this little one but your daddy is a mean man. He tried to keep me a slave when I was trying to escape with your momma. He is a bad, bad man."

Dawnalee looked confused and scared at which point Nanny could hold her tongue no longer.

"Don't you believe that honey child, your daddy is a good man, a real good man."

Nanny then turned her attention toward Leah.

"How dare you say that about Mista Jameson! You're poisoning this little girl's mind against her father. Her daddy is the finest man I ever knew and he would never have tried to keep you in slavery. There's not a bad bone in that man's body."

"What do you know? I was there, I know what those Hartford's did and he is one of them."

"I was there too, did you forget, and I tell you Mista Jameson would never have turned you in."

"He is no good and you should mind your manners around me. I'm family; I can have you thrown out of this house, so I think you should mind your own business and stay out of mine."

"Mista Jameson and Miss Delilah will never throw me out of this house; we're thicker than family. Besides, you're the bad person here. That man opened his house to you and your children, and you repay him by trying to turn his only daughter against him? Neither one of you do a blessed lick of work around here, all you do is live off that man's kindness and now you try to make him look bad to his daughter; shame on you, shame on both of you."

"I ain't talking to you no more."

"Oh yes you will and you will listen to every word I have to say. You get off Mista Jameson's back and leave him alone. You stop telling lies to his daughter or I will go to Miss Delilah and tell her what you are up to."

"Who you callin" a liar? My daughter will stand by me and take my side. I'm her mother."

"Miss Delilah will take Mista Jameson's side, he's her husband. You be careful or you will find yourself on the outside, you hear me?"

Leah started to walk away from Nanny, out the front door and into the yard.

"Don't you walk away from me."

Under her breath she muttered, "That woman is trouble, real trouble."

Nanny took Dawnalee by the hand and led her into the kitchen trying to explain to the impressionable child that her father was not the monster her grandmother painted him out to be. A large ginger snap cookie helped to ease the tension and put out the fire.

When Jameson finally came back down the stairs, another surprise awaited him; the one Nanny was hoping she would be able to forewarn him about.

"Hello Uncle."

It was his nephew, Jebediah, who had escaped jail in Boston and had threatened to kill him.

"You don't look happy to see me, I wonder why."

Jameson looked around for his gun, but he had left it upstairs.

"Don't worry, uncle, Madeline told me how kind you were to her and saved her from that soldier. She made me promise I would not do any harm to you; seems you have charmed another woman with your wiles."

"Jeb, if you want to kill me, just do it and get it over with, I am not up for a fight right now."

"No uncle, I've decided that what you have done here is very noble. These people all love and respect you and I want to be a part of it... if you'll let me."

Jameson looked suspiciously at Jebediah, not knowing if he should believe him or if it was just another lie.

"I know, I have to earn your trust and I fully intend to do that, if you will give me a chance and let me stay."

"You rebuilt the house, Jeb, you are entitled to stay, but how do I know I can trust you?"

"I will earn your trust, uncle. I want to start my life over again and be a decent human being. After all, if I wanted to kill you, I could have done it when you entered. I'm a different man, I've changed. Give me a chance to prove it, please."

"You will have to work, like everyone else."

"I'm prepared to do that, uncle, tell me what to do."

Jameson hesitated but decided to give him the benefit of the doubt and said, "Alright, Jeb, c'mon and I'll show you."

Jebediah lived up to his promise and worked hard to earn everyone's trust. Except for Delilah's mother and sister everyone seemed to get along. Blacks and whites working side by side, helping each other, it was just as Jameson had imagined. Too bad he never got the chance to prove it earlier; maybe the war could have been shortened or avoided altogether.

Delilah was hurriedly on her way to the office when she was approached by a woman draped in a long dark dress with a shawl covering her head. She slid the hood back to reveal her long black hair and striking green eyes suggesting she was not a local lady.

"Pardon me madam, my name is Sapphira and I have come quite a distance, all the way from N'Orleans. The townspeople suggested I speak to you. I am in search of a Frenchman who goes by the name of Michelle LeBrute. I have reason to believe he is in this town. Might you know of his whereabouts?"

Delilah gave her the once over and then asked if she was a friend of the Frenchman.

"Heavens no," she exclaimed, "I am here to extract retribution for what he did to me and my family."

Delilah was intrigued and asked the lady into her office and told her to have a seat.

"Tell me more," she inquired.

"Do you know him? Are you a friend of his?"

"Heaven forbid!" Delilah stated, "I am no friend of his."

"Good because he is a bad man, a very, very bad man. He pretended to love me all the while, behind my back, he was wooing my sister and unbeknownst to both of us was cajoling our mother at the same time. He managed to trick us all into lending, or rather stealing all our money then leaving us destitute to fend for ourselves while he ran off with yet another woman. I managed to track him here; at least I hope he is here. Do you know of this man?"

"Yes I do but I am not sure where you can find him. What do you plan on doing to him when you find him? Be careful his brother is the sheriff here, Mordechai LeBrute."

"I am of gypsy lineage and my family history delves deep into magic the black arts and potions."

"Go on."

"I plan on putting a curse on him."

Delilah let out a loud "Ha, I hope you are going to turn him into a frog or some such beast."

Sapphira laughed and said, "I see you have no love for this man."

"None, in fact I detest him and the sooner he is gone the happier I would be."

"If I did that I would not be able to get my money back, but I can still harm him."

"You might find him at the sheriff's office or at Taffeta's Gentleman's Emporium, a fancy name for the saloon; they seem to be his two favorite places."

"Thank you madam, I am most grateful."

"Be careful, he is fast with his sword and does not seem to value human life."

"I will, thank you for your help."

"Come back and tell me what happened. I will enjoy hearing him get what he deserves."

Sapphira laughed again and said, "I most assuredly will see you again."

She covered her head and disappeared through the door as Delilah ran to the window to view her departure.

Sapphira walked toward the sheriff's office but something, perhaps a sixth sense, led her to Taffy's instead, where she spied her prey sitting in a corner drinking and carousing with one of the ladies.

She entered and stood there glaring at him. Michelle instantly felt her presence and stopped his carousing. His eyes immediately transfixed themselves onto the mysterious lady. He quickly rose and ran in her direction trying to placate her.

"Sapphira, what a surprise, what are you doing here? I am so glad to see you."

He ushered her out the door and around the corner out of sight off the main street.

"I was going to send you a telegram to tell you where I was."

"Quit lying, Michelle, you are a despicable human being, you don't care about anyone but yourself. I'm surprised you even remember me."

"Of course I remember you, how could I forget such a beautiful lady?"

"I want all the money back that you stole from my family."

"I did not steal anything. You willingly gave it to me."

"You promised to marry me, and my sister and my mother."

"I could not do that; it would be bigamy, no?"

"I want my money."

"I don't have it mon cheri, I spent it… all gone."

"Then I will tell the law what you did."

Michelle laughed, "The law, the law is my brother. He will not listen to you. Go home before I hurt you some more. Some people are born to be eagles; others are born to be pigeons. Guess which one you are?"

Sapphira reached into her pocket and pulled out a vial that contained some white powder. She opened it and poured it into the palm of her hand. Speaking in a Cajun dialect, she mumbled a few words, lifted her hand to her lips and blew the powder into Michelle's face.

He coughed and swore at her, "What nonsense is this?"

"I have cursed you," she stated nonchalantly.

"Cursed me! I don't believe in such garbage, er, what kind of curse?"

She knew he was susceptible to her beliefs and started to toy with him.

"It will change you into the kind of animal that you lived your life as, in your case I would guess a rat."

"What, a rat, no, no, I don't believe you, you jest with Michelle."

She smirked at him and then decided to tell him the truth.

"You are right, the spell I cast says you will lose all your riches and you be killed by your own sword and by someone you love."

"Hah, that will never happen, I am too fast for that. Perhaps I will test it on you."

"You can't, the spell makes me immune to you and your sword."

"We'll see about that," he said as he reached for his sword.

For some reason he could not remove it from its scabbard. His hand could not grasp it. He became flustered as Sapphira laughed hysterically.

The Frenchman grew irate and kept fumbling for his sword but to no avail. He then lost his temper and threw his hands around her throat and tried to squeeze harder and harder but he could not seem to affect her.

He picked up a rock from the ground and tried to bash her in the head. Again nothing happened, in fact the rock crumbled and fell out of his hands.

"You are a witch, get away from me," he squealed.

Sapphira gloated and said, "Get me my money, you have 24 hours or I will do far worse to you, perhaps a pox or a plague."

Sapphira pulled another vial out of her pocket. This one contained an ominous black powder that seemed to burn in its own container. She glared at him as her green eyes took on an ominous glow. Michelle was visibly terrified and wondering what the powder would do to him.

She started to stroll away with Michelle groveling close behind, then turned and added, "Beware the black cat."

Michelle rather perplexed begged her, "What does that mean?"

Sapphira answered, "If I don't receive my money in a day, a black cat will cross your path and will know the time to meet your maker is nigh."

"Please cheri, I cannot raise that much money in such a short period of time. Please show me some mercy."

She ignored his pleas and sauntered to the hotel. Michelle tried to gain control of himself and clear his mind. He smiled that evil smile as an idea popped into his head, "*I cannot harm you but perhaps another one can, yes and I know just the fellow.*"

That night, Delilah was leaving her office for the evening and to her dismay ran into Michelle LeBrute.

"Hello cheri, you look lovely tonight, *cough, cough.*"

Delilah tried to hurry past him and completely ignore him, then she paused and inquired, "Michelle, what happened to that nice woman from New Orleans who was looking for you? Didn't she find you?"

"You met her? *cough.* "

Delilah shook her head in the affirmative, as Michelle searched for an answer, he was surprised at this turn of events and tried to cover up any involvement with the lady.

"Oh she had the wrong man, *cough, cough,* she was mistaken about me, she left town to find the true culprit."

"Sapphira was supposed to come back and see me before she left."

"What can I say; she must have been in a hurry, *cough cough.*"

Delilah just looked suspiciously at him and commented, "You have a bad cough there, I don't want to know how you caught it or from whom, just stay away from me, I don't want anything you have," and went on her way, not wanting to speak to him any more than was necessary.

She promised herself she would look into the matter tomorrow. Besides, he was sick and she thought, *perhaps Sapphira did, in fact, put a curse on the evil Frenchman.*

Michelle watched her saunter off as he grabbed for his sword and easily pulled it out of its case. He thought for a second then uttered under his breath, *"Rubbish on that gypsy and her curse."*


Meanwhile, something more malevolent was occurring at Serenity and Willow Hills; people were getting sick, with high fevers, coughing and convulsing. It started with one person, but had quickly spread and very few were recuperating. The disease was running rampant through the entire area. Anyone who caught it seemed to last only a week or two, and then succumbed to the disease. Doc called it some kind of flu, and said this was the worst outbreak he had seen in a number of years. He needed an antibiotic to try and fight the disease and only possessed a small amount, not nearly enough for this sized outbreak. He had tried to acquire more and sent telegraph messages to other towns. It seemed the disease was not unique to Willow Hills but had spread to every neighboring town and city. No one could spare any medicine. In fact, the medicine was becoming more valuable than gold and unscrupulous people took to stealing and hoarding it. It would be no easy task trying to find and obtain the elusive vaccine.

Scouts would have to be sent out in a kind of reconnaissance mission to find and acquire the elusive serum. There were few volunteers as everyone was frightened and rightfully so, this disease was a killer. Those who eagerly rode out limped back in a few days or weeks empty handed and completely discouraged. Whatever they found was not for sale, but worse than that, they heard tales of an armed group that was stealing what little vaccine there was and leaving a trail of death and destruction in their path. It looked hopeless.

Not sure of how the disease was spread, the populace took to folk remedies to try and thwart the onslaught. Was it mosquitos, ticks, gnats, face to face contact or airborne, no one was sure, not even the doctor. People would retire into their homes at dusk and not come out again until first light to avoid the supposed carriers.  Innovative individuals took to creating makeshift screens for windows using cotton fibers and stripped leaves nailed between boards to allow a breeze to pass into their homes but hopefully keeping insects out. It did not work all that well and deteriorated rapidly, especially in a rain storm.

Nanny, using an old recipe passed down through generations concocted a "skeeter" repellant from cedar, lavender and clove oil, mixed with fennel and thyme. It reeked and no one wanted to apply it to their skin, much to her displeasure.

"I know it smells that's what keeps the darn pests from biting you, they don't like it neither."

She splashed it all over herself and it seemed to work, no insects, animals or people came near her for hours.

"See, I done told you it works, now who's next?"

There were no takers, but they knew something had to be done before half the population was decimated.

# Chapter 11

## *Shaman*

The populace of all the neighboring towns, as well as Willow Hills, was frightened and worried about this new disease that was threatening their lives and the lives of their loved ones. No one knew when or where it would strike or who would be its next victim. Everyone was greatly concerned and getting very protective of families, turning their backs on anyone showing even the least amount of symptoms. A cough or a sore throat was a cause of great concern as the sickness spread rapidly. People were quickly quarantined and kept secluded until the doctor could examine them and determine if they were a risk or not.

Enter a traveling medicine show, with ring master, Brother Credence. He was neither a brother nor was his real name, Credence, but he had a way with words and could talk you out of your last dollar. He was rather stout with longish unkempt hair which he flung around when he delivered his sermon. He wore a long brown robe with a hood, which was cinched at the waist with a simple rope. He knew of the disease and was determined to prey on men's fears and ignorance. He traveled from town to town and brought with him an elixir that he touted could cure all ills; even the dreaded flu. His first phase was to walk all over town introducing himself and inviting everyone he met to come and see the show that night, assuring them that they would not be disappointed.  He visited all the shops and asked if he could place his flyers in their windows. Before he was done, everyone heard about the man and his miraculous cure.

The medicine show carriage was camped at the edge of town and the curious people were beginning to gather at dusk until there amassed quite a large crowd, almost everyone in town was there for the occasion, sans Delilah, who was too busy to bother with such silly nonsense. By the time the oration began, there was standing room only. Brother Credence was about to put on one amazing show, as the night fell on the hopeful multitude. He surveyed the crowd, threw back his long hair, took a deep breath and prepared to raise the dead. A voice, strong, loud and commanding sprang from the portly gentleman.

"Brothers, sisters, friends, welcome one and all. What you will see here tonight you will not believe, you will think your senses are lying to you, but I assure you everything is legitimately true. Do you suffer from aches and pains? Is it hard for you to get up in the morning? Does your back hurt? Do you have rheumatism or stiffness, swelling, inflammation? Do you just want to feel like you did ten or twenty years ago? Well then, I have the cure for all that ails you."

The crowd nodded and Brother Credence knew he had them in the palm of his hand. Everyone suffered from what he just so eloquently stated. Now came the proof, he called out into the crowd for people who were suffering and wanted relief. Several people held up their hands but he selected only two unfamiliar faces. People who said they had heard about the elixir and traveled miles just to see the healer and purchase his miraculous potion.

One man had a bad limp and could only hobble, but after partaking of Brother Credence's elixir, his leg regained its movement and he could once again walk. The crowd was astonished. It was inexplicable.

Next came a woman whose hands, it seemed, were badly cramped with arthritis, she could not straighten out her fingers. She also drank a glass of the serum and lo and behold, her fingers began to straighten out, right before their eyes.

Lastly and perhaps most amazingly was the person they all knew, Michelle Le Brute, who had a fever and a bad cough, reminiscent of the disease all the people were deathly afraid of contracting. He was hacking and wheezing as he carefully uncorked the amber glass container and slowly tasted the strange concoction, then took a few deep gulps and stood there for a moment. There was silence and then, astonishing as it was, but with one dose of the tonic he suddenly stopped coughing and his fever was completely gone.

He appeared to be healthy decreeing, "Sacra bleu, I am cured, I do not cough any longer nor have I a temperature, it is a wonder drug I have never felt better."

The three proclaimed it was a miracle cure and promptly bought their own bottles, praising Brother Credence all the time.

*"Could this be for real"*, the people thought, *"It must be; look what happened to all those people and we know Michelle Le Brute."* Then Brother Credence began to speak again:

"Brothers, sisters, friends, what you have seen here with your own eyes is just a speck of what my elixir can do. Yes, you will become believers when you take your first glassful of my tonic. I know, you doubt your senses and say this can't be true; it must be some kind of sorcery or witches brew but I assure you it is one hundred percent  pure. You cannot deny what you have seen here tonight. These people have been cured and are totally healed with nothing more than a glassful of my proven cure-all. You see friends, I worked for years to find the right ingredients that properly mixed together, would produce a stimulant that makes your body heal itself. Yes, you heard me; your body will heal itself when you use my magic elixir."

"What's in it?" someone yelled out.

"I'm glad you asked that question, brother, but if I told you then anybody could mix up a batch of my potion and put me out of business. No, I cannot divulge the ingredients, but I can tell you that it is one hundred percent natural and each and every ingredient is safe for human consumption. Now, I only have a limited supply and I have to go to another town tomorrow, to spread good health and save lives, so I can only offer you this delightful concoction for tonight only. I am not trying to become rich, no my friends, I am trying to help people, so for today you can purchase an extra-large bottle of Brother Credence's magic elixir for the low, low price of only one dollar. Yes, one measly dollar to insure your good health and well-being and to protect you from that dreaded fever ridden epidemic. Yes it will even cure that, I assure you, as I have seen it happen with my own two eyes. Now, I'm awaiting on you all, who will be the first to buy a bottle?"

The crowd pushed forward, everyone wanted a bottle. There were too many people and they practically begged him to take their money. Some brought two and three bottles, not taking any chances that they would get sick in the future.

Doctor Pritchard was not convinced and doubted that the elixir could really work. He purchased a bottle to conduct his own tests and to see what it actually contained. He opened the bottle, smelled it, and ascertained that it contained a rather large amount of alcohol. What else was in there, he was determined to find out.

"Now, take your bottles home and dose yourself with a large glassful tonight and you will wake up tomorrow healthy and hearty. Thank you my friends, you have emptied my wagon. I am sold out. God bless you all, goodnight, and goodbye."

When the crowds had dissipated, Brother Credence climbed back into his wagon and counted his windfall. He had made over three hundred dollars, but he was far from done.

He hitched the horses to his wagon and pulled out of town and out of sight and patiently waited as the people he supposedly cured turned up at his wagon. They were patsies, his friends, whom he hired to help him perpetrate his sham.

"Now all we have to do is wait a few hours and then we creep back into town and loot our customers. Ha, ha, ha," he laughed, as he removed his robe and put on pants and a shirt to avoid recognition.

The elixir was mostly alcohol with a powerful opium laced sedative mixed in and everyone who drank a large glassful would get drunk, drowsy and pass out, thereby allowing the shaman and his cohorts to sneak into their homes and steal all their valuables. The three would be burglars, had a few drinks of their own and patiently waited out the clock.

Soon it was time and the trio of thieves started back into town, each equipped with a sack to collect their booty.

It was late and most of the town was asleep, or passed out from the potent tonic. It was very quiet and they had no trouble picking locks, jimmying windows, entering houses and relieving the owners of their money, jewels and precious metals.

Delilah was working late, as usual, and was leaving for the night to return to Serenity when she happened upon the burglars. Each party was surprised by the other, and they quickly placed their hands over her mouth and tried to push her back into her office.

From across the street, a lone figure of a soldier noticed something was wrong. He could hear her muffled cries and proceeded to her aid.

What is going on here?" he demanded.

It was the soldier Delilah had seen before; the one who had abused her in the past and she had redressed in pubic on that very street. Now he was here to help her.

"Shut him up," Brother Credence whispered to his cohorts.

They attempted to grab him, but he was, after all, a soldier and quite distinguished in hand to hand combat. He fought them as best he could, but he was badly wounded in the war and only a shell of his former self.

Delilah was being held firmly by Brother Credence; he had one hand around her waist and one over her mouth. She kicked her leg up, as hard as she could, from behind connecting with the poor man's genitals. He shrieked and released his hold allowing her to break free and push one of the men off of the soldier. That was all it took for the warrior to gain the upper hand.

Brother Credence regained his composure and grabbed his sack, swung it, hitting the soldier and knocking him down, yelling to his friends, "Let's get out of here."

They grabbed what they had already taken and fled in opposite directions so as to confuse any potential followers. Delilah attended to the soldier.

"Thank you for saving me."

"I only wish I could have done more ma'am. Are you alright?"

"Yes, but who were those people and what were they doing?"

"I don't rightly know, perhaps we should tell the sheriff."

"Yes, I agree, let's go."

Delilah helped him up and they walked on over to Mordechai's office.

"You're the soldier I yelled at in the street for abusing me when I was a slave, aren't you?"

"Yes Ma'am, I am. Again, I am so sorry for whatever I did to you. I hope you can find it in your heart to forgive me. I know I don't deserve it but I have changed and deeply regret what I did in the past."

"Well you did come to my aid and if you have actually changed then I guess I can forgive you…but I don't think I can ever truly forget."

"Thank you ma'am, I appreciate it, and if we all remember the atrocities and never forget then evil like that can never happen again."

"Yes, I agree. What is your name sir?"

"John Stafford, ma'am."

"Well John Stafford, I'm Delilah Hartford, pleased to meet you."

"Pleased to meet you too, ma'am, it is an honor."

"Mr. Stafford, it is none of my business, but what were you doing up so late walking the street?"

"I can't sleep, ma'am. I keep reliving the war every time I close my eyes; I see all the bloodshed and death. I wish I could forget it all just for a little while so I could sleep."

"John, I remember all the horrors of being a slave also, but I try to think of the future and how it will be better for all my descendants, and everyone. Why don't you come see me tomorrow and I can give you a job, something to take your mind off what you have been through and maybe you will find peace, like me."

"Thank you ma'am, maybe I will, maybe I will."

They arrived at Mordechai's office, he was asleep. He had also purchased the elixir and had taken an extra-large dose. He could not be roused. At that moment Doc Pritchard entered the office.

"I heard someone scream, are you ok, Delilah?"

"Yes, thanks to this soldier here. Some strangers were running about town. They all had sacks loaded with something and scattered when we almost apprehended them."

Doc put two and two together and did not like the answer he was getting.

"Was one of them a heavy set man with rather long hair wearing a padre's robe?"

Delilah said he was large with long hair but was not wearing a robe. Doc deduced that it was Brother Credence and told Delilah and the soldier that the elixir they were peddling was mostly alcohol and an opiate disguised with a sugary taste and a cherry reddish color. He probably got eighty percent of the town drunk and when they passed out, the robbers proceeded to steal from them.

"What can we do about it, Doctor?"

"I'm afraid there is nothing we can do until morning when the town wakes up and realizes what happened. There are not enough sober people in this town tonight to get a decent posse to go after them. Perhaps they will all learn a valuable lesson from this."

They went on their separate ways waiting for the sun to illuminate the prior night's misfortunes and decadent choices.

The next morning, people woke to headaches and hangovers, not to mention the loss of their valuables. A posse was formed which combed the area, but to no avail, Brother Credence and his traveling band were long gone. To make matters worse, the tonic did nothing to cure anyone's ills; in fact, the influenza epidemic was still growing and still spreading with no end in sight.

Delilah returned home to find her mother coming down with the illness. It seemed to prey on the old, the young and the infirmed first, but no one was really safe. She was very concerned and did not want her mother to die the way her best friend, Martha Barrington had a few months earlier. It took her so long to find her mother that she could not bear the thought of losing her so soon. Nanny whipped up some old fashioned folk lore remedies and administered them to Leah but they only helped for a while; soon the symptoms returned and this time worse than before. Marcus and Ambrosia took turns tending to their mother so she was never alone, yet she was progressively getting worse. The disease would not be conquered. Then the unthinkable happened one night as little Dawnalee woke up complaining to her mother and father of a sore throat. She also had a mild fever, which is how the dreaded disease started. They were both very worried and tried to console the child as well as themselves, hoping for a miracle.

Doctor Pritchard could not locate a smidgeon of vaccine anywhere in the immediate area. He needed someone to go to a large city like, Richmond and try to acquire the vaccine. Marcus volunteered because of his mother; Jebediah, to prove he had changed and Jameson, when Dawnalee began to complain of a sore throat. The three unlikely musketeers left immediately on their quest.

There was an unsure air permeating the expedition. It was a matter of trust, neither man was sure of the intentions of the other man. When the chips were down could they be relied upon to help each other.

Jameson did not fully trust his nephew, Jebediah; had he in fact changed or would he take any opportunity available to get rid of his uncle. Jebediah was not sure his uncle would look out for him after all they had been through. And as for Marcus, the feelings were mutual, he disliked all white men and these two were no exception. If it came down to survival it would be every man for himself; yet they needed each other to find and bring back the life giving vaccine that would save their loved ones. The doubts were there although no one voiced them aloud. They would soon be tested and all the answers would be forthcoming.

# Chapter 12

## *Vaccine*

The three unlikely partners passed from small town to small town and in each locale, people were sick with the disease, some had quarantine signs warning visitors to avoid the town and move on. None of the small municipalities had any medicine and told the tale of how soldiers in confederate uniforms had come into their town and stolen all their vaccine, leaving them to suffer.

"What did they look like?" Jameson inquired.

"They were ex-soldiers who went by the name of Randall's Raiders. Some people tried to stop them but they were killed and then the town was set on fire as punishment. We were not strong enough to resist them."

"We thought they were our friends. They were southerners but didn't care about us at all."

Jameson and the others pushed on, knowing full well they were chasing a dream. Every town was suffering and every town was out of the vaccine. The trio began to grumble amongst themselves and differed in their ideas of which direction they should pursue on their quest. They thought of splitting up to cover more territory and vowed to ride harder and faster. Time was running out and days were being wasted in their search for the serum; until they came upon a town called Crooked River, the road to which had been blocked and was guarded by a man in uniform.

"This town is quarantined, nobody can enter," the guard said.

"Is everyone ill?" Jebediah inquired.

"No, everyone is healthy and we want to keep it that way, so get moving."

"Do you have any medicine?"

"We ain't supplying strangers with our medicine."

"We can pay for it. We have United States money."

"Yeah, let me see it."

Jameson showed him the currency and the gold coins.

The guard aimed his rifle at him and issued an order, "Now drop all that money right there on the ground and get out of here and I'll let you live."

Jameson stared at him in disbelief.

"If I were you I'd hurry before I change my mind."

Instead of dropping the cash on the ground, Jameson threw the money at the guard temporarily disorienting him as all three men went for their guns. The guard knew he had been tricked and was outnumbered so he dropped his rifle. Jameson dismounted and collected his cash. They tied up the guard, gagged him and left him there, which was kinder than what he had planned for them. Jameson quickly remounted his horse and they all rode peacefully away, but only until they were out of earshot of the guard.

"That must be the town that has all the vaccine," Marcus said.

"What should we do?" asked Jameson.

"We wait until nightfall, sneak into town, locate the vaccine, take it and slip out undetected," said Jebediah.

"I don't know," said Jameson.

"Look, uncle, it's a long way to Richmond and long way back. We will lose a lot of people if we don't do this, and besides they stole it, so it's not theirs, at least not legally."

"I agree, I'm not gonna let my mother die because of a bunch of robbers. Let's come up with a plan," said Marcus. "We'll create a diversion and be gone before they know what hit them."

"I don't know, it's too risky," said Jameson.

"C'mon Jameson, do you want your daughter to die because of these thieves?"

Jameson reluctantly agreed and they sat down to devise a plan.

The town was conveniently located in a valley with a river running alongside it on one side and a mountain on the other. There was only one road in and out of town that made it virtually impenetrable. How could they enter without being seen and get out without being captured that was the problem. They put their minds together and devised a plan. The river was running low and was traversable, so that would be their point of access.

Nightfall came and they tied their horses to a tree and slipped on foot across the stream and into the Town of Crooked River. They wondered where the serum might be and looked for the doctor's office. They crept up to the door. It was locked. Both Jebediah and Marcus knew how to pick a lock and just like that, the door was opened. They rummaged around and found some vials but where were the rest?

The doctor returned and was quickly muzzled so he could not scream.

"Where is the rest of the vaccine?" whispered Jebediah.

"I don't know," replied the doctor.

"Yes you do," insisted Marcus. "Your friends stole a lot of it from neighboring towns and it is here someplace, and you are going to tell us where it is or we will kill you."

Marcus pulled out a large knife, held it up to the doctor's throat and said, "I'm only gonna ask you one more time, where is it?"

Jameson tried to reason with him saying, "We have women and children dying in our town, we desperately need that vaccine. You took an oath to heal all people, not just these people. Will you honor that pledge and help us?"

The doctor nodded yes and willingly gave up the location; the saloon, but said it was heavily guarded and they would never get near it. That is where the diversion was to come into play.

They bound and gagged the doctor, to keep him quiet and assure the soldiers that he did not willingly help them. Marcus made his way to the other end of town by the blacksmith's barn. He freed and scattered all the horses so no one would be able to follow them and then he started a fire. He waited for it to spread out of control before screaming "Fire, Fire!"

People came running from all over and began a bucket brigade, leaving the saloon virtually unattended. Jameson and Jebediah snaked their way around the buildings and alleys and entered the saloon. There was one guard who was quickly dispatched by a blow to the head, and there behind the bar in a lock box was their reward, just as the doctor had said. There were two boxes and Jebediah wanted to take it all but Jameson insisted they only need the one and to not be greedy. If they left some of the vaccine, perhaps the renegade soldiers would not give chase; at least he hoped. They grabbed their prize and ran out the back, down the alley and out to the waiting horses. But, where was Marcus, he should have been back by now.

"Let's go," said Jebediah.

"I can't leave without Marcus."

"We have to get this back before they realize what happened and come after us."

"I know, but I can't leave him. You go and we'll catch up."

Jebediah hesitated, wished his uncle good luck, turned his horse and galloped off. Jameson reluctantly crept back into town to find a man who did not even like him and would probably have left him behind if the tables had been turned.

Marcus, it seemed, was caught trying to escape after he started the fire and was being interrogated by the man everyone called, Captain Rip. Marcus was trying to convince them that he found the fire already burning and was trying to alert the town, but no one was buying that story. They decided to try harsher methods and were readying the hot tar and feathers to coerce him into confessing. Jameson knew this Rip Randall meant business and was capable of anything.

He snuck back to the doctor's office and found him still bound and gagged. He untied the man and told him, what they were going to do to his friend and he needed the doctor's help once again. Using the good doctor as a shield, Jameson walked out onto the street and up to the where they were holding Marcus. With a kerchief placed over his mouth so the soldiers would not recognize him, he demanded they let

Marcus go or he would kill the doctor. Then another thought occurred to him and he started to cough and complain of fever and not feeling well. The town panicked, fearing he had the disease and would spread it throughout their town. They urged the captain to cut the black man loose and let them go. He reluctantly relented and Marcus was freed. Together with Jameson and the doctor in tow, they started to back out of the town, telling everyone to stay where they were or the doctor would be killed.

One of the captain's men had circled around and came up from behind. He placed his pistol in Jameson's back and commanded him to drop his gun or he would kill him. Jameson knew, he had been outmaneuvered and was about to drop his pistol when a shot rang out from behind. He felt the gun that was pushed into his back suddenly fall away and the once threatening man fell to the ground. He briefly turned around to see the welcome sight of Jebediah who had returned with their horses. They quickly mounted them, let the doctor go and galloped off into the night.

"This is not over, we will find you and you will pay," was the threat they heard as they disappeared out of sight. The townspeople had to find their horses and by the time they did, Jameson, Jebediah and Marcus would be long gone.

Marcus said, "Thank you for coming back for me, Jameson, I was wrong about you. You could have left me there to die, you didn't."

"Well let's both thank, Jebediah. He could have left both of us there to die. I guess you have changed, Jeb."

Jebediah smiled and said, "Let's just get this serum back and save some people."

The three men forged a strong friendship that day, realizing that they were not so different after all. They were feeling their oats and referred to themselves as the Three Musketeers, laughing all the while as they rode off into the forest.

Back at Serenity, Leah and several others were succumbing to the disease. Their breathing was labored when they could manage to take a breath. Dawnalee and Ruby Rose had also contracted the infection and neither Nanny nor Delilah could do anything to help. They applied cold wet cloths to their heads and gave them doses of Nanny's homemade remedy, but nothing seemed to help. There only hope was the vaccine and it could not get there quick enough.

Back on the trail, the men were riding all night and were exhausted, but dare not stop. The horses were fatigued and sweating profusely. They decided to give them a rest, after all a dead horse would be of no benefit to them at all. They built a small fire and cooked some of the food they had, to keep up their strength. They were discussing the crime they had committed that day, robbery was bad enough but they had also killed a man which was punishable by death, but they did it to save human lives; did that make it alright. A crime is a crime regardless of the reason. They just had to avoid being caught. No one knew who they were or where they came from so for the moment they were safe. They just had to get back to Willow Hills before the disease took another life. An unexpected rustling in the brush alerted them to visitors, unwelcome visitors.

Three men approached them on horseback and asked them if they could rest awhile by their fire. Reluctantly, they agreed, but it was an uneasy meeting; each group watching the other with suspicion.

"What are you doing out in these parts?" the strangers asked.

"We could ask you the same question," said Jebediah.

"This is our land and you are trespassing on it."

"We only stopped to rest our horses, we'll be going soon," said Jameson.

"What's in the box?"

"That is none of your concern."

"I think it is. Three men riding fast through my property holding on to a strong box; maybe you all are bank robbers."

"We are not bank robbers."

"Then show us the contents of the box."

Jameson, Jebediah and Marcus decided to show them and try to avoid any further confrontations. They opened the box to reveal syringes and bottles filled with a brownish clear liquid. As the three strangers gazed at the contents, the other three put their hands on their guns and waited.

"It's a vaccine to fight the flu epidemic. Our friends and family have it and are depending on us to get it back to them before it is too late."

The three strangers looked at each other and nodded.

"We have family with the same disease. You give us that box and we let you live, otherwise…"

"We can't do that. We risked our lives to get it and we're not going to simply give it to you."

"We can't let our families die either and there is no other vaccine available for miles around."

It was a stalemate, as the six men eyed each other deciding what action to take. Jameson, Marcus and Jebediah whispered to each other and all nodded in agreement.

A compromise was proposed, "We can either shoot each other in which case no one wins or we can give you some of the vaccine; but in return you switch horses with us. Ours are too tired to continue and we need to get home fast. Since you are close to your town, there is no need for urgency and you can ride our horses at a slow pace."

The three strangers looked at each other, mumbled inaudible words and agreed to the terms. More bloodshed had been averted. The booty was divided up and civility returned to the frightened constituency. They switched their belongings from one steed to the next and were once again riding at high speed to save their loved ones; hoping they had saved enough of the drug to treat everyone who had come down with the disease.

Riding through the night and part of the next day, they finally arrived back at Serenity and Doctor Pritchard immediately began to administer the antidote. For some, it was a lifesaver, for others it was too late.

Leah's fever was high and her lungs were filled with fluid. Her breath was labored and she had to fight for each gasp of air. Marcus ran up to her.

"I came as fast as I could mama. I tried, I really tried," cried Marcus.

"She knows you did all you could," said Ambrosia, "Don't blame yourself, you hear?"

To everyone's surprise, Leah called for Jameson. He knelt down next to her, expecting another berating, but she had other thoughts.

Something needed to be said so, gasping for each breath, she began, "Jameson, my son, I'm sorry for all I've done to you. You are a good man and a good husband to my daughter and a good father to my grandchild. I know now you had nothin' to do with me bein' recaptured. Can you forgive this old woman for bein' so stubborn and blind?"

"Of course, I forgive you, Leah, I'm just glad you had a chance to reunite with your daughter and granddaughter."

She abruptly grabbed his arm and pleaded, "Call my children to me, please."

Her three children rushed to their mother's side as her voice grew weaker and she whispered, as best she could, in between wheezing for breath, "My prayers were answered. I got to see my little girl again and my dear grandchild. Now the good Lord is calling me home where I'll have peace at last. Be good my children til we all see each other again in heaven."

Delilah, Ambrosia and Marcus were by her side as she breathed her last. There suddenly was a warm breeze that wafted past the three mourners and over Leah's body. It disappeared as quickly as it had come and brought tears and reminiscing to Delilah. She had felt that breeze before, in Martha Barrington's room, when she had passed on. It somehow brought a peace to the grieving family.

Delilah, Ambrosia and Marcus were holding onto each other, weeping for their mother when Dawnalee, cried out for her mother. Delilah ran over to her and held her close to her bosom, telling her, "Mommy's here, everything will be ok."

"Her fever broke, I think she's gonna make it," Nanny said.

"Thank God," Delilah prayed, "and Ruby Rose, come here, let mommy hold you too."

She felt cool and seemed to have no fever, Delilah looked at Nanny inquiringly.

"Yes, she's okay."

People were responding to the drug and most were getting better. They had survived the disease and triumphed, but there was a price to pay and almost everyone in town had lost someone. It brought the people closer together and that Sunday, at services, they all thanked the Lord for rescuing them.

Leah was buried on the plantation, next to Delilah's first child, Eve, who had been cruelly murdered by the evil overseer and Jebediah's mother. Her friends and family delivered a rousing version of a gospel tune as a tribute and a remembrance to her and all the other souls lost to the fever.

*"Bring me home, Lord, Lord, bring me home.*

*Welcome me, Lord, Lord, with open arms.*

*I been workin' and slavin' on this land too long,*

*Bring me home, Lord, Lord, bring me home."*


After the funerals and a brief period of mourning the community returned to work and their normal everyday lives. Life and death were accepted norms, people lived and people died. That was life and you lamented for your loved ones, but there was work that had to be done to ensure the survival of those who were left and someone had to do it, so it was back to the daily routine.

Delilah remained closer to home for a week or two and then the call of work beckoned her back to town, but she vowed to keep sensible hours.

She returned to find that there was trouble in one of her shops. It seemed John Stafford was not getting along with the rest of the staff. Delilah had tried to get him gainfully employed but it was not an easy task. John suffered from what would now be called post-traumatic stress syndrome. He constantly relived the war in his mind and sometimes had trouble distinguishing between the past and the present. She gave him a job in one of her stores but his bad temper flared up constantly and resulted in fights with the other workers and customers. She tried him in the stock room, loading and unloading crates and boxes, but he got upset when deliveries were late or not complete and again started fights with the delivery men. She placed him in the lumber business thinking perhaps physical labor would cool his temper but all it did was inflame him all the more.

Delilah sat down with him and asked him what he would like to do. He was not sure as his attention span wandered and he appeared to be in a daze or in some faraway place into which she could not reach him. John Stafford's mind returned to the battlefield as it had done many, many times before. There he was with his comrades charging up some hill that some captain thought was important and ordered it taken or retaken once again. The men charged as rifles crackled and exploded all around them from both sides. Then came the booming sound of cannon fire, too numerous to count, which suppressed even the sounds of the gun fire. The large balls plowed through the standing soldiers like bowling pins in an unprotected alley and landed somewhere in the distance behind him. In all the furor, John Stafford accidently tripped in a mole hole and as he fell to the ground, felt the breeze of a large projectile pass right next to him. He looked up to find all his friends either gone or torn to pieces and he, the sole survivor. Panic ran through his body as he knew death was just seconds away for him also, unless he could think of something fast. He lie motionless staring up at the clouds and pretended to be dead as the onslaught of Yankee soldiers came rushing past, down the hill and on to victory.

John laid there for what felt like an eternity before all the smoke and noise subsided and he felt safe enough to move. He rose to his feet and tears welled up in his eyes as he surveyed the carnage. In a few seconds, he finally broke down and sobbed uncontrollably. Why did all those men die and why was he left alive? Should he have done something more, was he a coward for pretending to be dead and not shooting more Yankees? The scene played and replayed in his mind over and over again. He felt tremendous guilt as if he had let down his comrades and his beloved south, but he also desperately wanted to live.

He struggled to find his way back to another fighting unit while avoiding northern caravans, subsisting only on berries and creek water. He lost a lot of weight and there were times when he thought he would not make it and had merely survived the battle to simply die in the wilderness. When he finally made contact, he was told the war was over and the South had lost, which made John Stafford feel all the more guilty of surviving. He would carry that guilt with him for the rest of his life. Nothing Delilah or anyone else could say or do would change the past or ease his mind. This was the lot of many of those poor souls, sad as it was.

He seemed to come out of the trance and return to the present time. He looked humbly at Delilah and told her he was useless and a worthless cause and she should not worry about him.

Any other employer would have simply written him off but not Delilah, she was determined to reach him and give his life some kind of meaning. She was however running out of options and as a last resort placed him as her bodyguard, a position she invented just for him. All he had to do was stay close by her and keep her safe, especially from that Frenchman, Michelle. Everything seemed to be working out alright until two workers, one black and one white were arguing about who was doing more work and should get more money. The little spat gradually grew into a shouting match and then one shoved the other and the next thing you know they were hitting one another. Delilah was called and John followed.

When they arrived at the scene, Delilah hollered, "Stop it this instant."

John ran into the fracas and pulled the two warring parties apart.

"Missus Hartford said to stop it and you will obey her," he ordered.

They told him to mind his own business and went at each other again. John temporarily lost it and pulled the two apart again, this time hitting them and throwing them against the walls, screaming and threatening to kill them.

Delilah ran up to him and grabbed him in an effort to stop the onslaught. He turned around and grabbed her by the neck and started to choke her, then realized who it was. He loosened his hands, looked at her frightened face and begged for her forgiveness.

Everyone was staring at him as he looked around in shame, covered his face and ran out the door.

Delilah regained her composure and ran out after him.

"John, John, stop and talk to me."

She dare not grab him again.

He turned and said, "Missus Hartford, I'm sorry, I can't be trusted. I don't know when I'll lose it again. I appreciate everything you tried to do for me, but I have to leave. Please don't ask me to stay, if I hurt you I would never forgive myself. Just let me alone, please."

Delilah said, "If that's what you really want, I'll do what you ask; but know this, if you ever need anything you can always come to me and I will always help you, understand?"

John shook his head as Delilah removed a few dollars from her purse and pushed them into his hand. It was a large sum of money and he wanted to refuse it but she insisted.

"This is for the work you have done and a little something more because you deserve it. I will not take no for an answer."

He smiled and placed the money in his pocket, then turned and walked away to confront his demons in his own way. Delilah only watched and wished she could have done more, perhaps one day he would return.

One particularly hot night on Serenity, Jebediah, unable to sleep, strolled outside and spied a figure dart into the barn. He went to investigate and there in a corner trying to hide under a bale of hay, Jebediah found his mother.

Bethany Sue had gone mad when she inadvertently killed her husband by slicing through a saddle strap on his horse. She was trying to keep him home while he wanted to ride into town each evening to find love at Taffy's emporium. She did not mean for him to fall off the horse and die, and never forgave herself, instead reimagining Jameson to be her husband. She was diagnosed as mentally ill and sent to a hospital. She must have escaped because there she was hiding in a corner of the barn like a trapped animal.

"Mother is that you?"

"Who are you? Stay away from me."

"It's your son, Jeb, Jebediah."

She stared, but did not recognize him, perhaps because of the facial scarring from the fire.

"It's me, I swear it is."

She looked closer and slowly approached the figure, staring at him in the moonlight.

"Is it really you, Jebediah?"

"Yes mother it is me."

"Oh my, it is you."

He hugged her and she unsurely put her arms around him in response. Bethany Sue looked disheveled and had a wild gaze in her eyes. There were twigs in her long matted hair and dirt on her clothing, she desperately needed a bath. Her finger nails were long and sharp and she had a strange stench all around her. He was ashamed that his mother had come to this and he had not been there to help her.

He smiled thinking she was alive and safe when she added, "I can't wait to tell your father. Josiah will be so surprised to see you. He lives in this house with that black whore and he thinks I should be in an asylum, so I hide out here in the barn."

"Mother that is Uncle Jameson, not daddy."

She looked bewildered at the surrounding area.

"How did you get out of that hospital?"

"The Yankees came and bombs were exploding and the place was in chaos, so I just walked out. I didn't know where to go so I came back here, but the place was empty. I knew about the passageway so I used it to go in and out waiting for your father to return and now he is here. Oh son, now that you are here, I'm sure he will take me back and get rid of that black hussy."

Jebediah was concerned and did not know how to handle the situation. He knew Jameson and Delilah had no love for his mother so he was forced to tell her to remain in hiding until he had a chance to discuss this with his wife and uncle. She agreed. Jebediah kissed her, brought her a blanket, some food and water to drink and tried to make her as comfortable as possible. When he was sure she was alright he went into the house to talk with Madeline. This would not be an easy problem to solve and could cause irreparable damage to his renewed relationship with Jameson and Delilah.

Relating the whole story to his wife was not easy as he too was guilty of ignoring his mother being ashamed of her and her illness. Madeline immediately insisted on seeing Bethany Sue and tried to ease her suffering but was rebuffed by the confused lady who viewed her as an enemy. She also realized the predicament they were in and vowed to help her husband break the news to Jameson and Delilah in the morning or at a safer time.

# Chapter 13

## *Randall's Raiders*

The day started out quiet in Willow Hills, but it would not last. Ample hoof beats signaled the arrival of Randall's Raiders. It was a group of a dozen rebel soldiers led by Captain Rip Randall, along with a wagon whose contents were covered with a tarp. He rode tall in the saddle, clad in his spotless grey uniform, wearing a hat with a large peacock feather stuck in the band. He had steely blue eyes that never lost their gaze. His men, followed obediently behind, waving the confederate flag proudly, ready to follow any and all orders, without question. They each sported the double R patch on their sleeve signaling their loyalty to their captain.

When they received the news that Lee had surrendered to Grant, they refused to believe it and decided to continue their private war. They roamed the countryside supposedly defending the confederacy and its way of life. They administered justice as they saw fit, mostly against northerners and blacks. They were really a band of renegades, and criminals, dispensing death and destruction as was witnessed by all who came into contact with them, including Delilah and Jameson.

They rolled into Willow Hills for two reasons and promptly stopped at the sheriff's office. The captain dismounted and strode inside. He stood there at attention glaring at the sheriff.

Mordechai looked up at the commanding figure and replied, "Yes, what can I do for you?"

Mordechai knew who they were and feared for his life and the town he had sworn to protect.

"I'm Captain Randall, you remember me?"

"Yes, how could I forget, what do you want?"

"I expected a warmer reception, sheriff, after all we did you a big favor when last we met; we did away with that despicable group of Yankees. That was a grand day for the confederacy. But today I am here for two quite different reasons; first, I'm looking for one of my men. We traced him here from other towns. I gave him a month for some needed rest and he never returned."

"Maybe he deserted."

"Not likely, sheriff, He enjoyed being in my army, besides he knew the penalty for desertion… death. Have you seen him? He would have been wearing a corporal's southern gray uniform with a double R patch on his sleeve."

"A lot of people come and go through this town wearing uniforms, especially with the war being over."

"So, you haven't seen him?"

"No captain, I have not," Mordechai lied, knowing this was the man his half-brother had killed a few months ago. "You asked me about him before and I told you then that I had not seen him and nothing has changed since that day."

"Other towns were persuaded to tell us where he went and they all pointed to your town, sheriff. People I have interrogated have recalled seeing him in your town. He must be here somewhere or someone knows where he went."

"Sorry, I cannot help you; maybe they just lied to save their lives."

"Well then how about, three men who came to my town, Crooked River, and stole a supply of vaccine from me?"

"Don't know anything about that either, sorry," Mordechai again lied.

"You know what we are capable of doing, if you are lying, don't you Sheriff?"

"I have heard and I still don't know anything."

"Then you don't mind if I look around, do you?"

"As long as it's peaceful."

Captain Randall just laughed and exited the building. He told his men to spread out, check the stores and ask everyone if they saw the corporal. He would check the saloon.

"Meet me at the tavern when you have finished questioning everyone."

Mordechai Le Brute checked his gun to be sure it was loaded; he hoped he would not have to use it. He rose and walked outside to see the soldiers canvassing the town. *This is not good*, he thought.

Captain Randall proceeded to Taffeta Jones Gentleman's Emporium, checking up and down the street for any clues.

He entered the saloon and asked for the owner; Taffy came out to meet him.

"Morning Ma'am, I'm looking for one of my men. I have reason to believe that he was in this town."

"I see a lot of men captain; you'll have to be more descriptive than that."

"He would have been wearing a corporal's uniform, grey of course, double R patch on his sleeve."

"A lot of soldiers come through here captain, after a while, they all look the same to me."

"Well then what do you know about three men stealing a vaccine to treat an epidemic disease that was threatening these parts?"

"I know of the disease, some people had it, some died. It seems to be gone now. Sorry I can't help you any further, now if you don't want to spend any money, I'm gonna have to ask you to leave."

One of the patrons, who had a little too much to drink, sauntered up to see what all the fuss was about and asked the man his name.

"I am Captain Rip Randall."

The man halfheartedly saluted the captain while slurring the words, "Rip, sounds like a dog's name to me. Here Rip, come here boy, play dead Rip. Good boy, that is funny," the drunk said as the crowd erupted into laughter.

The captain pulled out his pistol and without a moment's hesitation shot the man, asking him," Now you be the dog and play dead, how funny is that?"

Silence fell over the entire establishment. Taffy told one of her girls to run and fetch the doctor.

She looked at the captain and said, "What is wrong with you, he was drunk."

"No one makes fun of me ma'am, no one. It undermines my authority."

The captain's men had been crisscrossing the town looking for their comrade and the thieves, but no one was willing to help them. Everyone pretended they knew nothing, remaining loyal to their town and the man and woman who saved it. When one of the soldiers entered the office of Delilah, he was surprised to see a black woman sitting there.

"Get your boss, girl, I want to talk to him."

She glared at him and said, "I'm the boss, what do you want?"

"You, you can't be the boss, you're …."

"Colored? It's a new world soldier, get used to it."

"You can't talk to me that way."

"I can and I will."

"You better learn your place or I'll have to teach you some manners."

Delilah slid her hand carefully under the counter and grasped the pistol she had hidden there.

"You will not teach me anything, but perhaps you will learn a valuable lesson."

The soldier was becoming quite perturbed by this insolent black woman and said, "The last time a colored girl tried to refuse me some pleasure, I forced her, then the rest of the men enjoyed her and then we tarred and feathered her to teach her a lesson and left her on the side of the road. Now you don't want me to do that to you, do you?"

"Are you the people who did that to a woman on the road to Charleston with her little girl watching?"

"That was us. We figured to teach the little girl a valuable life lesson she would never forget."

"You horrible excuse for a human being, how could you do that to a poor woman and with her little girl watching it all; you're nothing but pieces of dirt."

"Now you're getting me mad, girl."

Delilah pulled out the gun and was ready to end his miserable life when another soldier came running through the doors saying, "The captain wants to see us right now."

"You're one lucky girl, but don't think I will forget this; I will be back."

He ran off as Delilah quickly went to the window to see what was going on.

The doctor was brought into the saloon but was prevented from attending to the bleeding man until all the captain's questions were answered, to his satisfaction. The doctor claimed he knew nothing and they only used the vaccine they had on hand to fight the influenza epidemic. He was finally allowed to aid the wounded man.

All the soldiers met up again at Taffy's as the captain had ordered and he bought them a round of drinks as they told him of their findings: no one knew anything or no one was willing to talk. They all denied any knowledge of the corporal or the vaccine. There was not a single traitor in the whole rural community.

"I smell a rat in this town. Somebody knows something but no one is talking. We need to make an example of someone, put a little scare into them so their tongues will loosen up. Now who shall we get as a volunteer? Let me think."

The captain looked around the town, eyeing the town's people one by one, looking for the weak link. He noticed the school and led his men in that direction. He walked into the classroom and saw the black and white children sitting and learning together and was appalled.

"Is this why we fought and lost so many men? Teacher, come here," he demanded.

One of his men ran over and grabbed Madeline, dragging her over to the captain. The children were visibly upset and began to stir in their seats and whimper. He pulled Madeline outside and questioned her about his missing comrade.

"I don't know anything sir, I swear."

He held her by her hair and told her to pick a child she wanted him to punish.

"I can't do that sir; please they are all good children. Leave them alone, please."

"If you don't want to pick one, then I will. Bring me that little colored boy with the plaid shirt," he ordered.

His command was promptly obeyed.

"Please leave him alone, please," Madeline begged, "Make an example of me if you must."

Mordechai was running toward the school, yelling; "Stop that, stop that now."

The little boy was crying as the captain held him close. Mordechai pulled his pistol as the entire group of soldiers drew theirs, and aimed them right at the sheriff.

"I can't let you hurt him," said Mordechai.

"Even if it means your death?"

"Yes," Mordechai reluctantly replied.

"I have no intentions of killing him, just maiming him a bit unless you tell me what you know about my corporal and my vaccine."

"We told you, we don't know anything."

"I don't believe you. We just came from another town whose residents were more than glad to tell us about the three men from this town who gave them some vaccine for fresh horses. They took a little persuading but they confessed to their crimes. Now I want the names of those three men or would you rather I have my men burn your town down to the ground. Would you prefer that choice, instead?"

"I don't want any trouble, but I have to stand up for my town, even if I die."

The captain slowly removed his pistol as if he were going to surrender then in an instant aimed and fired it at Mordechai, sending him to the ground. He released the boy and turned to his brigade and said, "Burn it, burn everything to the ground."

Mordechai whispered to himself, "Heaven help us all."

People were running, screaming through the streets, in panic. The soldiers ran to the wagon and uncovered bottles of oil, a keg of tar and torches. They started firing their guns, breaking windows, and kicking in doors. They were going to destroy Willow Hills.

The soldier who had threatened Delilah earlier returned with his pistol at the ready.

"I told you I'd come back to settle the score."

Delilah readied her gun, aiming to shoot the soldier if he made another move.

"You better be accurate with that pistol, girl."

"Don't worry, I am."

"You shoot me and other soldiers will come running, you won't be able to stop them all."

"But you won't be alive to see it."

The soldier thought long and hard about that predicament. He wanted to teach her a lesson but was not ready to die as a result. For the moment, it was a standoff.

In the ensuing melee, a voice called to the captain, "You don't have to do that. I have all your answers. Call off your men, captain and I can deliver to you the men you want."

The captain turned to see the Judas; Michelle Le Brute.

"What do you know?"

"I know a man named Jameson Hartford killed your corporal, and he along with two others from his plantation went to your town and robbed your vaccine. "

"Tell me where I can find them and I'll stop this destruction."

"He lives on the Serenity plantation, a few miles out of town down the east road."

"Why are you telling me these things when no one else would?"

"I hate to see unnecessary destruction, and I have no love for Hartford. Your corporal was getting, shall we say, friendly with Hartford's niece and he did not like it. A fight ensued and Hartford killed him."

"You better be telling me the truth or I will come back and you will beg me to kill you."

"I am not lying to you Mon Captain."

The captain fired his gun into the air twice, as a signal to call off his men. They all came running. Delilah was safe again, at least for the time being.

He stood for a moment looking a little perplexed then peered at the sheriff lying in the street and said to him, "Hartford… isn't that also the name of the black lady who was running all the businesses in this town? Didn't I tell you to remove her from that position? I hope you did because when I'm finished with her husband I'll be back to check on that and there will be hell to pay if you have not fulfilled my request."

The captain ordered his men to mount up. Off they galloped, holding the stars and bars proudly, heading toward an unsuspecting Jameson and a vulnerable Serenity.


The town went into fire brigade mode and quickly doused the few fires that the soldiers had started. Mordechai was carried off to the doctor's office and his half-brother Michelle went to visit him.

"He was shot in the chest but the bullet missed any major organs; he will survive," said Doc Pritchard. "Let him rest ok?"

"Yes, of course, doctor, and thank you for everything," Michelle said, as the doctor left.

"What did you tell them that made them leave?" Mordechai asked his brother.

"I told them Jameson Hartford killed their corporal and stole their drugs."

"How could you do that? They will kill him and…oh that is your plan, they kill him, you get his grieving wife. That is low brother, even for you. I can't let you do that. Help me up so I can tell the people to go help him."

"No brother, I will not and neither will you. No one is to know what I did; besides I did it for you and the town. What is one man compared to my dear brother and my adopted hometown? Just rest and let my plan run its course."

"No, you have to try to help him. He's a good man. They'll murder him."

"Yes and I will have his rich widow as my own," he laughed.

Mordechai tried to get up and yell for help, but Michelle pushed him back down and then took his gun and said he would shoot him again if he did not listen. Again the sheriff pleaded with his brother and tried to yell for help.

Michelle said, "Forgive me brother," and struck him with the butt of his pistol silencing him for a while. No one was going to interfere with his plan.

The townspeople also were wondering what happened and why these renegades left in such a hurry. They gathered in the street to discuss the matter.

Delilah came to join them, when Madeline rushed into their midst and said, "I heard the captain say he was going to the Hartford plantation to even the score."

Delilah in a wide eyed panic asked the people to get their weapons and ride with her to Serenity. Whoever was capable, agreed and the mini posse was formed and quickly headed out, but the rebels had quite a head start.

# **Chapter 14**

# *Payback*

The sound of the approaching army was thunderous, kicking up dust and debris as they entered Serenity, riding tall in their saddles with their rifles held at attention. All the employees in the fields and in the nearby housing stopped to see the impending horde. The renegades pulled up to the house and half the men dismounted their horses.

Nanny looked out the window and said, "I don't like the looks of this Mista Jameson."

Jebediah thought they had come for him as he deserted the army about a year ago. Jameson told him to remain inside, then they both suddenly recognized the intruders; Randall's Raiders.

"Don't go out there, uncle."

"Stay in here, Jeb; get a gun and keep me covered."

Jameson exited the front door.

"Are you Jameson Hartford?"

"I am."

The captain's men quickly grabbed him and held him.

"I find you guilty of murder and thievery. What do you say to that sir?"

"I don't know what you are talking about. Who did I supposedly kill?"

Dawnalee and Ruby Rose were playing in the back of the house and came running forward to see what all the commotion was about.

Ruby Rose took one look at the men and screamed, "They killed my mommy, help me, help me."

One of the soldiers ran up to her and screamed, "Boo little girl, I'm the boogey man."

She started to run away when Jameson screamed at them to go into the house. Nanny came out to get the children, gave a dirty look to the captain and said, "You better get off our property, you have no rights here."

The captain laughed and said, "Teach her a lesson in respect."

One of the soldiers went over and backhanded Nanny, who just stood her ground and continued to glare at the attacker.

"She's tougher than she looks, captain, should I give her another?"

"No, let her be, we're after thieves and a murderer, I don't care about her."

Jebediah emerged from the house pointed a gun at the captain and demanded, "I think you should leave now or I will be forced to kill you."

They had underestimated the captain as his men had already spread out and one had worked his way up behind Jebediah disarming him and knocking him to the ground.

"Are there any more heroes here?" asked the captain. He waited and looked around, then added, "I guess not."

One of the soldiers whispered to the captain who said, "I see we have the second thief in custody now. Where is the third, the colored man who helped you?"

There was silence.

"Well we have ways of making you talk."

"You didn't answer me. Who am I supposed to have killed?" asked Jameson.

"You killed my corporal in your town."

"I did not."

"You killed him because he was getting friendly with your niece."

Jameson thought back, and then remembered the incident.

"It's true I had an altercation with him but I did not kill him that was someone else."

"Who?"

"A man in town."

"It was the Frenchman," said Jebediah, "He stabbed your corporal."

"Now that's a predicament. He's the one who told me it was you."

"What! That conniving snake, he said that because he wants my wife and figured he'd have you do his dirty work for him. You kill me, and he thinks he can force himself on her."

"Well that is interesting and after I deal with you, I'll go back and kill him, so you don't have to worry about him after all. However, you did steal from me and my town and you have to pay for that."

Jebediah countered, "You stole that vaccine from other towns so if we are thieves, you are a thief also. It wasn't yours to begin with."

"Possession is nine tenths of the law and I possessed it so it was mine. I have to teach you both a lesson that nobody breaks Captain Rip Randall's laws and lives to tell about it. This type of discipline has a way of being retold throughout the countryside so others will learn and fear us and never cross us, ever!

He turned to one of his men and said, "Heat up the tar, get it nice and hot. We're gonna make us some ducks. His men all snickered. You should be very worried gentlemen; the tar will stick to you and will burn your flesh, right down to the bone. It will hurt a lot, but only for a while, until you pass out from the pain. If you're lucky, you'll die."

He laughed as they tied the two men to a tree and stripped Jameson and Jebediah of their shirts. Nanny begged him for leniency for her two friends but it fell on deaf ears.

The two little girls ran out into the fields telling the men and women that Jameson and Jebediah needed help. Marcus took charge and ordered the men and women to gather their tools as weapons and to follow him. He told them to block off the roads so the soldiers could not easily escape.

"Knock them off their horses and then it will be an even playing field. I will try to kill the captain first, maybe that will scare the others into surrendering."

The fire was raging and the tar was boiling as the soldiers dipped their brushes into the gooey liquid, ready to spread it over the poor men's bodies. They taunted the prisoners by waving the tar covered clubs close to their bodies and laughing.

"Do it slowly men, I want them to feel all the pain."

The workers ran up from the fields and were ready to charge, knowing some of them would not survive; guns against farm tools were no match.

Suddenly, Bethany Sue came running out of the barn screaming and wailing, "Don't hurt my Josiah. Get away from him."

She was acting erratic, running and screaming, jumping and howling. She looked like an eerie apparition that no one had seen the likes of before. The horses were spooked by the sound and appearance of the unstable woman. They reared up on their back legs and whinnied knocking the captain and some of the other soldiers out of their saddles and alarming the soldiers already on the ground.

The workers sensing an opportunity charged the confused and addled soldiers. Only a few shots managed to be fired as the workers overpowered the soldiers, showing them no mercy. Jebediah and Jameson were freed and joined in the fight. The soldiers seemed confused by the attacking workers, they thought this would be an easy task, but they were completely overwhelmed and out maneuvered, for the first time in their lives, and by a bunch of farmers. A pick to the body and a scythe to the neck can be more damaging and much more painful than a bullet. The soldiers were outnumbered and were attacked from all sides. Unable to steady their aim, rifles were being used as bats and were quickly severed in two by axes. Those who tried to run found the escape routes blocked and also fell victim to the angry workers. It seemed as if the farmers were like a horde of locusts coming at them from all directions and completely devastating the chaotic soldiers. They did not know who to shoot first so most of the shots were never fired. One was cut down, then another, then another; they did not stand a chance. As each soldier fell, the remaining ones panicked further, despite the captain's orders to stand and fight.

Some of the militia maneuvered their steeds down the road in an effort to regroup, increase momentum and once again gain the upper hand as some of the farm workers eagerly pursued them. From over the horizon, the townspeople emerged riding at a fervent pace in an effort to save their own. Viewing their options, the soldiers decided to charge the approaching townspeople and hope for an escape route. As one of the soldiers neared Delilah's horse, he recognized her as the lady from the store he had threatened earlier.

"It's you! Well this time you will learn respect," he mocked as he went for his pistol and eagerly planned her demise.

Delilah, however, was at the ready and fired her pistol first hitting the combatant square in the chest, knocking him out of the saddle. He lay there looking shocked and dismayed as his life's blood poured out onto the ground.

The rest of the soldiers did not fare any better as they became trapped between the workers and the town posse. They soon succumbed to the same fate. They were no match for the angry united citizens of Willow Hills.

Perhaps sensing defeat, the captain was forced to retreat backwards toward the wagon and his horse, all the while trying to defend himself with his sword, keeping the angry mob at bay. In the confusion, he fell over the back of his cart and was pinned in place against a tree. The tub of hot tar spilled and the gooey sticky residue poured out of the barrel and flowed all over him, almost covering him completely in the black lava. He screamed and screamed until he was smothered in the black ooze and death finally brought him to the fate he had earned. The other soldiers all lie on the ground, dead or severely injured. The mini war came to a quick and just end.

Delilah jumped out of the coach and ran into Jameson's arms. They kissed and hugged each other. Madeline ran over to Jebediah and did the same.

"Are you alright, James?"

"Yes, I'm fine. They didn't get the chance to finish their revenge, thank God."

"I'm alright too," said Jebediah, reassuring Madeline.

Little Dawnalee and Ruby Rose were praised for their bravery and quick thinking. They would get an extra big slice of apple pie for dessert that evening.

They thanked all the workers and the townspeople for their help and praised them for working together to defeat the evil soldiers.

"This is now a holiday; take the rest of the day off, rejoice and relax. You should all be proud; we have come together as one and destroyed a common enemy. We can live and work side by side and help each other in times of need. We are truly a community."

Smiles were abundant all around and everyone was gratified, hugging and wildly shaking hands with congratulatory accolades.

Doctor Robert Pritchard, together with Nanny tended to the wounded. Luckily, there were no casualties, but some were more seriously injured than others. Bullets were removed, bandages applied and miraculously all were patched up and told to get some needed rest, which they did.

Doctor Pritchard sidled up to Jameson and slid an envelope directly into his hand. He said he did not know where it came from; he found it on his desk that morning with a note directing him to please deliver it to Jameson Hartford at his earliest convenience. Jameson placed the envelope in his pocket, vowing to read it later.

The soldiers' dead bodies were loaded onto their own wagon and Jebediah said he would bring them into town and deposit them right at the feet of the sheriff.

Then came the topic of Bethany Sue; Jameson and Delilah were surprised to see her. Jebediah and Madeline apologized for not telling them, but he was afraid they would not want her there and he did not want her sent back to the asylum.

"I can't be mad; she kind of saved our lives," Jameson said.

"Did you forget what she did to me, James? I don't want her here," Delilah stated.

"We can't just throw her out, Lilah."

"If she is staying, then I am leaving. Make your choice."

Jameson hesitated.

Delilah vehemently defended her stand. "She had my baby killed. She tortured me and you defend her?"

"I'm not defending her, Lilah, wait, Lilah."

She ran off into the house with Nanny in close pursuit.

Jameson looked at Jebediah shrugged his shoulders and said, "I'm sorry, but what she did to my wife is hard to forgive and forget."

"Let her stay the night Jameson and we'll move her in the morning, please," Jebediah asked.

"Let me see if that is alright with Lilah."

Meanwhile, in the house, Nanny was telling Delilah, what was on her mind.

"Miss Delilah, you are wrong. What she did happened in a different world, let it go. We can't live in the past."

"I can't Nanny."

"You told everybody else to forget the past and live and work together, but you don't take your own advice."

"Nanny, she had my baby killed."

"Then think of your husband and child. You been working so much, they hardly ever see you anymore."

"I have to work. There is a lot of pressure on me, people rely on me for their livelihood, besides, I'll never be poor again. I won't be under anyone's thumb ever again."

"You're going to lose your husband, if you keep this up. I see how unhappy he is and how much he loves you and wants you with him."

Delilah thought for a moment, as Jameson entered the room.

"Lilah how about if she just stays tonight and we move her someplace in the morning?"

"How can you be so insensitive to me?"

Delilah's fury flared up again, forgetting what Nanny had just said to her.

"I guess you made your choice. It's clear to me who is more important in this house. I'll be in town! When she leaves, let me know, maybe I'll come back, maybe."

Delilah was playing her card, an ace in the hole; calling Jameson's bluff, hoping he would fold and send Bethany Sue away. Again, he hesitated and that was all she needed. The angry woman left in a huff while Jameson called after her and looked helplessly at Nanny. He could see the faces on the other people. He again felt like half a man, being dictated to by his wife. He ran after her and tried to reason with her, but she would not hear it; boarded her coach and headed back into town, leaving a distraught Jameson to bear the cross himself. He watched helplessly as her coach left the plantation and disappeared down the road. He vowed he would clean himself up and go after her later after supper.

The rest of the family retired into the house and enjoyed a good meal prepared by the best cook in South Carolina, Nanny. Poor Bethany Sue wanted to eat by herself and preferred her fingers to any utensils.

Jameson said he would be going into town to settle once and for all his account with Michelle. It was bad enough he would not leave Delilah alone, but now he deliberately lied and sent those soldiers to kill him. It was time to settle the score once and for all with that evil Frenchman. Nanny told him to wait until the morning as Delilah needed some time to cool off and confronting her tonight would only inflame an already volatile situation. He reluctantly agreed.

The matter of Bethany Sue was debated and Jameson decided to leave it up to Jebediah as she was his mother. Bethany Sue was still confused and thought Jameson was her husband, then looked at her son, Jebediah and thought he was her husband. She was still in need of medical help and Jebediah said he would take her to the doctor in the morning, and see what therapy he recommended.

Bethany Sue may have looked like she was in a daze but she was eavesdropping and heard all the discussions and vowed to herself that she would not return to that so called hospital. She concocted a plan to escape, should it be necessary. She also resisted all efforts to clean her up or wash her; she did not trust anyone and would not let even Madeline touch her. They persuaded her to don a new cotton nightgown, but that was the extent of the changes she would allow.

After dinner, everyone retired to their respective rooms for a well-deserved rest. Bethany Sue preferred to stay on the couch planning for a quick getaway should it become necessary.

Alone in his room, Jameson pulled the envelope out of his pocket and tore it open. The card simply read: Please come see me at your earliest convenience, we have to talk, signed Abigail.

*"What could she possibly want?"* He thought. *"I'll see her tomorrow before I go into town,"* he supposed and retired to bed, thinking nothing more of it.

Michelle witnessed Delilah's return to Willow Hills and overheard the town talking of the death of the soldiers and how Jameson had survived. Michelle was disappointed with the results of his treachery and that his plan was foiled. He would claim he did it to save the town and his half-brother. Surely they would understand that he was looking out for them. He also knew Jameson would come for him; it was a matter of pride. Perhaps he would be able to kill him in self-defense. He would have to be careful; he did not want Delilah to blame him for her husband's death, as he wanted her and her money. It would all have to wait for a while; it was Jameson's move, for now he had better make himself scarce. Besides he had other things to attend to and surreptitiously crept out of Willow Hills.

# Chapter 15

## *Swamp Monster*

It was the middle of the night and everyone was asleep, well almost everyone. Bethany Sue was awake, dressed and determined to leave before her "husband" was able to send her back to that so called hospital. She crept down the hall and almost made it out the door, before she was spied by little prying eyes. Dawnalee and Ruby Rose were hungry and had their minds set on another piece of that apple pie. They knew if they asked Nanny or their father, the prize would be denied; so there they both were looking in the cooler for the pie as Bethany Sue was trying to sneak past them.

"Hello, who are you?"

Bethany Sue was startled and answered, "I'm, why I'm your gramma."

"My gramma; I met my gramma and you're not her. She went to see God and is not here anymore."

Bethany Sue shook the cobwebs out of her head and stuttered, "I I mean I'm your aunt dear, your auntie Bethany Sue."

Dawnalee was confused, but proceeded with her cross examination of the stranger.

"Where are you going?"

"I have to leave; I'm not welcome here anymore."

"Who wants you to leave?"

"Your father and I think my son."

"I like you; I think you should stay."

Bethany Sue was touched and tears filled her eyes as she hugged the little child.

"Want to have some pie with us?"

"No, no darling; you both should be in bed."

"You won't tell anyone, will you?"

"No sweetie, I would never do that. You go back to bed now, and we won't say anything more about tonight, okay?"

She kissed Dawnalee and Ruby Rose and stepped out into the night. The air was warm and moist as was usual in South Carolina at this time of year. Knowing they would come after her if she stayed on the road, Bethany Sue walked into the surrounding woods and headed south. She had traversed the woods and swamp many times before and felt confident that she would elude detection.

Dawnalee and Ruby Rose watched as their auntie passed into the forbidden forest; they grabbed a big slice of the gooey sweet apple pie and decided to follow her outside.

Dawnalee yelled in a whisper, "Auntie, you're not supposed to go into the woods. Mommy and daddy said to stay out of the woods. They will be mad."

Dawnalee started to follow her as Ruby Rose said, "Dawnalee, you shouldn't do that, you're gonna be in trouble."

"Don't tell anyone Ruby Rose, I'll be right back."

"Dawnalee, come back, I'm scared for you."

Undaunted, Dawnalee pressed forward.

Bethany Sue did not realize she was being followed and kept pushing onward, deeper and deeper into the woods. The air was thick and the ground was wet. She was heading into the swamp area which the workers created from cutting down too many trees when the plantation, adjoining housing and logging business were being built. It was rumored that many people got lost in this area and were never heard from again.

Suddenly she stopped, believing she heard a tiny voice and thought she was imagining things again and hearing people that were not there. The voice was getting closer and louder. Bethany Sue began to panic and picked up a large branch to defend herself if it came to that. She looked in the direction of the voice and a small figure emerged into the clearing, it was Dawnalee.

"What are you doing here child? You should not have come."

"You're not supposed to be in the woods either, auntie."

"I better take you back home, darling."

She was panicked and took the child in her arms. "*Now they will blame me for kidnapping*", she thought as she started to walk back to the mansion.

Dawnalee was concerned with the stories of the swamp monster, a half human, half animal creature that supposedly stalked this area and fed upon those unlucky enough to be trapped here. Bethany Sue tried to put those fables to rest saying she had been in these woodlands many times and had never encountered someone like that, telling the child not to believe everything she heard as the truth.

Bethany Sue started hearing noises again and not sure if they were real or imagined began moving erratically through the swampy region, stopping, turning and going in a different direction until she was completely turned around and had no idea how to exit the dreary swamp. The earth beneath her feet was wet and muddy and caused her to stick to the ground with every step she took. The deep mud kept pulling at her shoes until they finally came off and left her barefooted, and at the mercy of the many snakes and creatures which called the swamp their home.

The voices grew louder and closer forcing Bethany Sue to seek refuge behind a tree, telling the child to be still and not make a sound. They were real, people were approaching through the muck, carrying sacks and speaking to each other, one with an accent she had heard before; it was French. *Who were these people and why was a Frenchmen in this horrible place?* She decided to follow them in the hope that they would surely lead her out, unless they were on their way in and then they would take her deeper into the swamp. Again she was confused and just sat there for a moment to try to figure things out. Dawnalee was cradled in her arms with her eyes and mouth covered to keep her quiet.

The group came to a stop and began a loud discussion.

"This is a good spot. Let us divide up the spoils."

Michelle Le Brute stopped by a large oak tree. Spanish moss was dripping down from its branches and clinging to anyone who was close enough for it to touch. Joining him was Brother Credence and two of his cohorts in crime. There was a large hole dug in the ground next to the trunk and dirt piled high with a shovel tucked in it. They dumped the contents of the sacks onto the ground. Bethany Sue was surprised to see jewelry, money, watches and all sorts of silver and gold items tumble onto the earth.

"This is a great place; no one could find us here. They are all too scared to come into the swamp," said Brother Credence.

"Where is the cash?" inquired Michelle.

"Cash was not part of our bargain. We agreed to split the stolen items with you. The ones we took from Willow Hills," said the man.

"Well I am changing that agreement; I didn't help you fleece all those lambs in Willow Hills for a measly quarters worth of some trinkets. I want half of everything in exchange for my silence… and protection from the law."

"Why should we give you half of what you had no part in getting. You did not help us rob those other towns," said the woman. "We agreed to cut you in on the take we got from your town only, not on everything."

"I need the cash, I will be leaving this town very soon, with someone very special and I need to travel in style and fast."

"I didn't know you were ready to settle down."

She doesn't know it yet either but that is irrelevant, I want half of everything you took or I will tell my brother, the sheriff, and the law enforcement officers of every place you have cheated."

"No, no we will not stand for it," said the man. "We don't have to take this. There are three of us against one of him;" said the man "Isn't that right, Credence?"

Brother Credence was silent.

"What's the matter with you? Tell him we are not going to stand for this."

Brother Credence apologetically replied, "Look, the influenza scare has ended and people are becoming skeptical of my elixir. My reputation is preceding me and it is getting harder and harder to sell my wares. I decided to retire and I need the money. You understand, don't you?"

"I understand you are a double dealing rat."

"Looks like you better turn and run or you won't be leaving this swamp," Michelle stated with the utmost confidence, as the man reached for his rifle and started to raise it.

"It is always the hard way with everyone, isn't it?"

As he pointed his weapon, Michelle displayed his agility with the sword and drew it out at lightning speed, not only dispatching the weapon of the attacker, but cutting off the tips of his fingers in the process.

He screamed in pain and yelled, "What is wrong with you?"

"Perhaps you have made me change my mind and I will dispense with you altogether."

"What? That is not fair," the man shouted, as blood oozed from his wounds

The lawbreaker looked at Brother Credence hoping for an alliance, all the while holding his bloody hand.

"Let's get out of here," the man said, but Brother Credence did not move.

"Are you with him or us?"

Again Brother Credence was mum. Michelle raised his sword and said, "Say goodbye to your wretched life."

He was no match for Michelle and was mercilessly pierced through the chest falling to the ground as blood spewed from his wound and quickly covered the ground.

The Frenchman then turned his attention to the woman who hastily turned and ran whimpering like a scared cat, yelling, "Traitor, I will get you for this, you turncoat."

Michelle looked at Brother Credence, who said, "Now we can get down to real business and split this booty two ways."

Michelle only laughed and waved his sword at the pompous shaman saying, "Put all the items back in the sacks and throw them into the hole."

Brother Credence hesitated as Michelle, with his sword at the ready, ordered him, "Do it now!"

"Are you trying to cut me out of this deal altogether?"

"Cut is such an appropriate word; just do what I tell you or I will use that word on you."

As he was obeying the order, he inquired as to why he was burying all the ill-gotten goods. Michelle did not answer him until he was done, then he told him to cover the sacks with the loose earth that was all around the hole. Again Brother Credence obeyed, but kept on questioning the Frenchman.

Screams were heard in the distance, leaving all to wonder what had become of the fleeing thief.

"Perhaps she is the victim of the swamp monster, Michelle laughed. "Keep going, forget her or you'll be next."

Brother Credence was visibly nervous but he obeyed and completed the task.

Michelle smirked and said, "I have decided to keep everything for myself and if you tell anyone, I will deny my knowledge and you and your friends will hang for your deeds."

"You won't get away with this."

Oh but I will. Don't forget my brother is a sheriff. Who will they believe a con artist or an upstanding citizen?"

"Are you forgetting I helped you get rid of that gypsy girl?"

"I appreciate you for taking care of that little matter for me."

"She told me what a wicked person you were and that you would deceive me, but I did not believe her. She also managed to put a curse on me before she died, saying  a trusted friend would betray me; now it appears she was right in her prediction."

"Just do as I tell you and everything will be fine," Michelle reassured the doubting Thomas.

Brother Credence pondered the dilemma he seemed to have gotten himself into and wondered if Michelle LeBrute would let him leave the swamp alive, after all he knew where the treasure was buried. He needed a trump card.

As the sweat poured from his oversized body, he said, "Did you forget about the cash? Let's talk."

"Yes, tell me where you hid all that money you took from all those unsuspecting little pigeons," Michelle said as he waved his sword menacingly at the fake healer.

"Don't do anything rash, Michelle; we can work this out like two gentlemen, besides if you want the cash, you will have to make a deal with me. You don't know where I have hidden it."

"That is true, but I think I can persuade you to tell me where you have stashed it."

"I will never tell you. If I did, I would have no bargaining chips left and you could just kill me."

"I would never do such a thing to my dear friend. Now tell me where the money is hidden."

"I don't trust you. Let me go and you can have all the treasure, I'll be content to keep the cash."

Michelle slashed his sword at the fraudulent brother and put a gash in his face, followed quickly by another on his arm.

"Watch out, you could seriously hurt me."

"That is the general idea. Tell me where you hid the money or the blade will come closer and closer to you with each swipe. Tell me now!"

Brother Credence realizing he probably was not going to get out of the swamp alive took the shovel he held in his hands and swung it at Michelle, narrowly missing his head.

"That was too close for comfort my portly friend. Be careful."

Brother Credence pretended to give in and looked as if he was lowering the shovel to the ground, then whipped it upwards, catching the unsuspecting Frenchman in the stomach sending him to the ground. Brother Credence raised the shovel to place the pointed spade directly into his supposedly helpless victim but the wily Michelle retaliated with his sword and ran it through the fake healer's body.

"What have you done, I'm bleeding, and badly."

"Maybe you could use some of your magic elixir, no?" Michelle laughed.

Brother Credence fell over gasping for air before he finally succumbed to the wound as Michelle just watched and waited for the inevitable.

"Oh dear, now I will have to find that foolish friend of yours and persuade her to tell me where the cash is hidden."

Bethany Sue gasped and made a muffled scream which alerted the Frenchman.

"Who is there?" he demanded, as he began to walk toward her.

Bethany Sue panicked and got up and began to run, leaving Dawnalee behind. She did not get very far when a hand grabbed her and pulled her backward toward him.

"Who are you?" he demanded.

She stared at him not wishing to answer. Little Dawnalee came running up, not wanting to be left behind in this unfriendly place. She did not realize the danger they were both facing.

He looked at the child and said, "Well aren't you the Hartford's child, Dawnalee, I believe?"

"Yes sir, I am," she replied.

"This is my lucky day; the gods must be smiling down on me."

"And who are you?" he said turning to Bethany Sue.

She thought he must be a friend as he knew the child and perhaps those were bad people. She told him who she was and how they came to be lost and how she would very much appreciate him helping them to find their way back home.

"So no one knows you are here?" he asked.

"No, no one."

An evil demeanor came over the Frenchman as he hatched his next plan.

Michelle thought to himself: *"This must be the mother of Jebediah, the one they say is crazy. I can use that against her. I can take the child, kill the old lady, blame the swamp monster and return the child to her mother. Delilah will be so happy; she will change her mind and fall in love with me."* He could not let her go as she witnessed him killing Brother Credence. He could not risk her telling everyone. Michelle was not worried about Dawnalee relating the account as he would just call it a fairy tale made up by an over imaginative child. Surely they would believe him over a child. Two people telling the same story would arouse suspicion, but one child, no one would pay her any mind. One could not help but wonder who was really mentally unstable, Michelle or Bethany Sue.

He grabbed the child from her aunt and pushed Bethany Sue away, telling her to run, the men in the white coats were coming to take her back to the sanitarium.

"Run, run quickly, they are almost here."

He pulled out his sword and said, "I will try to protect you, now run."

"Where I don't see anything?"

"They're right there, don't you see them."

"No, no I don't see anything."

"They are almost upon you, run."

I have to take care of the child."

"I'll take care of her, run quickly, see, they have the straight jacket ready to put on you."

He took a swipe at her with the sword, cutting her arm, pretending to be fending off the doctors. She panicked, shrieked and ran off. It was not very difficult to cause illusions to return to the old lady's already fragile mind. The evil Frenchman knew that and played upon her weaknesses. Dawnalee began to cry for her tormented auntie.

"Don't worry little one, Michelle is going to take you home to your mommy, Okay?"

He put Dawnalee down and told her, "You stay right here my little dear, first I have to go help your auntie, Okay?"

Dawnalee was scared and started to run back in the direction from whence she came, she was not as disoriented as her aunt.

The Frenchman was dismayed, he wanted to silence the old lady, but did not want to lose his chance to impress Delilah by returning her lost child. He reluctantly gave up one chase and instead ran after Dawnalee.

Ruby Rose had awakened her father and told him about the old lady and Dawnalee going into the forbidden forest. Jameson quickly dressed, woke Nanny and told her to round up a search party. He was going into the swamp to find his daughter.

He was out the door and with a lantern and started into the forest exactly at the point where Ruby Rose showed him the two had disappeared.

"Dawnalee, Dawnalee, where are you?" he kept shouting, "it's your father, tell me where you are."

Dawnalee heard her father and ran toward the voice screaming for him. Michelle was in hot pursuit and also following the voices, determined to not lose his chance for redemption.

Dawnalee could see the lantern and ran toward her father. Michelle also saw the light and tried to head her off, but he spied Jameson and stopped just inches short of grabbing the child. Jameson would not look so kindly on him for any reason and he knew it, preferring to avoid the conflict and try a different tactic to win Delilah. He slithered back into the swamp, determined to clean up his mess and continue his search to silence Bethany Sue.

Dawnalee ran a few more yards and straight into the arms of Jameson. He hugged her; then scolded her for going into the forest. She told him what happened and about the scary men and that other man; but most important was that auntie was still in the swamp. Jameson, Jebediah, Marcus and some of the workers ventured into the forest, trying to follow the large footprints, hoping to find Jeb's mother.

They searched and searched, managing to stay in constant view of each other so as not to get lost. They called out her name, but there was no reply; they could not locate Bethany Sue; but traces of blood indicated something bad had happened. Marcus tripped over something, and upon bending down unearthed two shoes, which Jebediah recognized as belonging to his mother. The frantic search was continued, now certain that Bethany Sue was somewhere in this horrible place.

They came upon a strange log cabin home which contained a fireplace with still glowing embers; hanging in it was a large cauldron which contained some kind of stew. In the other corner was a bed of leaves and twigs and a blanket made of animal pelts. Someone or something lived here and could not be far away. Still they kept looking, but to no avail.

It was dangerous as the swamp contained poisonous snakes in the trees and water which nipped at their boots but luckily were not able to penetrate the thick leather. Alligators would raise their heads out of the dark gloomy water, watching and waiting for a chance to catch their morning meal. Then there was the quicksand, which was everywhere, every step had to be carefully planned.

They went off in a different direction and found some recently unearthed ground. There was an awful lot of blood and they wondered if something or someone was buried there. Since they had no tools, they dug with their hands, deeper and deeper, until they uncovered some canvas bags which contained jewelry and money. Could this be Willow Hill's possessions that were stolen by Brother Credence? They took the bags with them and after a few hours, Jebediah decided to call off the search; she could not have gotten this far into the swamp and survived. Sadly they all returned home. Jebediah would get the sheriff, more men and return to comb the area hoping to find his unstable mother.

Michelle was nowhere to be found. Hearing the strangers and knowing what he had done, he quickly slipped away into the darkness and mist.

What had happened to Bethany Sue and who were the people Dawnalee kept talking about? Why were the sacks from the Brother Credence robbery buried there? Whose blood was it? There were too many questions and no answers. They would have to go into town and tell the sheriff and hope he had some answers or at the very least a solution. They needed to organize a search party and try again.


Jameson was glad that Dawnalee was alright but very annoyed that her mother was not here. If something had happened she would be the last to know. He was getting more and more upset and pacing around the house muttering to himself.

Nanny finally said to him, "Mista Jameson, you should go into town and get Miss Delilah. The two of you need to sit down and work this out before it gets any worse, you hear me?"

He looked at her and nodded yes.

"Well then get goin', what are you waitin' for, go?"

He kissed little Dawnalee and Ruby Rose goodbye, nodded a big thank you to Nanny and whispered, "Wish me luck."

"You don't need luck; you got love, true honest to goodness love."

"Bring Mommy back with you daddy," Dawnalee pleaded.

"I will try, sweetheart, I will try."

Jameson ambled out to the barn and hoped that there was still enough feelings left between them to reclaim his one true love.

# Chapter 16

## *Unexpected Consequences*

Jameson saddled up his horse and Jebediah boarded the wagon. Each was going into Willow Hills with a separate agenda. Jebediah was delivering the dead soldier bodies to the sheriff, along with the bags of stolen property and asking for a search party to go into the swamp and look for his missing mother. Jameson was going into town to settle the score with Michelle and to bring his wife home. The two men started out together but Jameson veered off and decided to stop at Tall Oaks to check on the two sisters, Abigail and Anabelle and respond to the note he held in his hand.

Abigail was pleased to see him and invited him into her home.

Jameson stated, "I got your message but I can only stay a minute. I have to go settle a score with that Frenchman."

She looked rather nervous and a little ill.

"Are you alright Abby?"

"Jameson, there is something I have to tell you. I wasn't sure whether to tell you or not, but I thought you should know."

She hesitated and then added, "I guess there is no easy way to say this, but…I am pregnant."

Jameson was shocked and blurted out, "Is the baby mine?"

"Of course the baby is yours, I'm not Annabelle; I don't sleep around."

"I'm sorry, I just meant… well you know we had a hard time conceiving when we were married and now all of a sudden, one night and well… how could that have happened?"

"Jameson, you know how it happened, and it only takes one time."

"I don't know what to say."

"Don't say anything, I know you're married and I can't have you, but I am going to have the baby and I'm going to keep it."

"Abby, you will be ridiculed by the town."

"I don't care; I've made up my mind."

"Who else knows about this?"

"No one, not even Annabelle, I've kept it a secret. Only Doctor Pritchard knows and you can rely on his discretion."

"Well, I won't just leave you. I'll help with the finances and raising the child and such."

"What will your…wife say?"

"Your wife, why Jameyson, your wife is probably having a good time right now, with that Frenchman," intoned Annabelle, who just sauntered into the room.

"You don't know what you are talking about, Belle," Jameson angrily replied.

"Abigail, why would you keep such a secret from me, your little sister?"

"Stay out of this Anabelle."

"Jameyson, why don't you get rid of that colored girl and remarry, Abigail. You can even have me on the side; two for the price of one."

Shut up, Annabelle."

"Oh please, Abigail, every man dreams of having two women at his beck and call. This is your golden opportunity, Jameyson."

Jameson was furious, "Abby, I'll speak to you later. I have to leave before I forget I'm a southern gentleman and say or do something I will regret later." Abigail ran after him and tried to call him back, but he rode away. She returned to the house and confronted Annabelle.

"How could you do that? What is wrong with you?"

"I only did it because I care about you. I don't want you to have to raise this child alone."

"You stay out of my life and away from Jameson, do you hear me?"

Annabelle walked away, but she was infuriated at Jameson for scorning her and making her sister pregnant. She vowed she would get him divorced to right the wrong he had perpetrated on their family name.


Jebediah arrived in town before Jameson and immediately dropped off the bodies of Randall's Raiders and the bags of merchandise they found in the swamp. He told the injured sheriff of their adventures and his missing mother. It turned out these were, in fact, the items stolen from the town and several other towns by Brother Credence and his cohorts. The sheriff wanted to investigate Bethany Sue's disappearance, but was still recuperating and unable to go into the swamp. He apologized, and offered to try to get some men to comb the swamp, but there was something else bothering the lawman.

Jameson rode into Willow Hills and was next into Mordechai's office. He complained of Michelle's lying and sending Randall's Raiders to kill him. He wanted revenge. Mordechai said he had not seen his half-brother since earlier that day and did not know where he was, but would speak to him when he reappeared. Yet there was another dilemma, the circuit judge was in town for only one day so Jameson was reluctantly re-arrested and would have to stand trial, today! It seemed the only thing that would be addressed that day was the complaint against Jameson.

The news spread rapidly and when Delilah was informed of the impending hearing she quickly went into action, calling on all her friends and employees. The witnesses who had filed the original complaint 5 years earlier and were still alive were called into the sheriff's office, as well as the hundreds who wanted to testify on Jameson's behalf. The small office was overcrowded in seconds, spilling out onto the street, as each waited his turn before the judge.

When the trial commenced, no one was willing to testify against Jameson. Those who had originally brought charges recounted their testimony and one by one dropped their charges. After all, it was Delilah and Jameson who had single handedly rescued and revived the town. Without them, the people would be poor and starving; besides that it was a long time ago and in reality, it was self-defense. Jebediah, an eye witness, even testified that Jameson was just defending himself and there should be no repercussions.

Michelle was hiding out and trying to incite the crowd to persecute Jameson.

"Don't forget, he killed your relatives. He should not go free. He has to pay for his actions. Your dead relatives and loved ones would want you to make him pay for his deeds. They would want retribution. You can't just let a murderer go free."

No one would listen to him and he became frustrated and infuriated that all his plans and actions were for naught and his arch enemy Jameson Hartford was still free and in the way of his goal of acquiring his wife and her money. Again he melted back into the shadows and faded out of sight like the devil himself.

The farcical trial quickly came to a close and all charges were dropped, Jameson was a free man again. He thanked everyone for their honesty and out of the jail he walked, to applause and handshakes from a grateful town.

Now he had to do something much harder; he had to face Delilah and tell her of Abigail's pregnancy. They walked hand in hand back to her office and Jameson sat down in a chair next to her.

"Is Bethany Sue gone yet?" she asked.

Jameson filled her in on what had happened during the night and how they did not know the fate of Bethany Sue.

"Is my baby safe?"

"Yes, she is fine. You should have been there."

"I know and I may have overreacted. Thank heaven my baby is okay, but as for Bethany Sue, I don't care, James, I have no feelings for her."

"I know."

"I have to get some things done, but I promise, I'll be home later, okay?"

"Delilah, there is something I have to tell you."

He only called her Delilah when it was serious, so she gave him her full attention.

"What is it, James, are you alright?"

"You remember that night I came here and found that Frenchman trying to seduce you and we had a fight and you said you would be ready to leave with me in an hour. I went to Taffy's to have one drink and three hours later, along with too many more whiskeys, you were still here working. I came by and saw you and I got mad all over again that you forgot about the time and me, yet again. I got on my horse and tried to ride home. I was drunk, very drunk and I lost my way and wound up at Tall Oaks."

"You wound up at Abigail's?"

"Yes, but I did not even know I was there. I thought I was home. I don't remember too much but I woke up the next morning in bed…her bed."

"You slept with her?"

"I don't really remember, but yes I guess, I did wake up in her bed."

"Tell me you didn't have sex with her too, please."

Jameson looked down, he could not face her; he was so ashamed.

"You had sex with her, your ex-wife?"

"Lilah, I'm so sorry, I did not know what I was doing, I swear."

"That doesn't make it better."

"I know, I know, but it didn't mean anything to me, honest. I only want you, but I'm tired of sharing you with this job and never seeing you and getting so mad when I see that Frenchman making passes at you."

"I never encouraged him."

"I know, and I am so sorry."

"Who knows about it, just you and her?"

"Well until today… now Annabelle knows."

"She'll spread it all over town."

"Oh Delilah, my dear, that's not the worst of it."

"You didn't sleep with her again, did you?"

"No, but… she says she is pregnant… and I'm the father."

"What, James how could you do that to us?"

"I'm so sorry, I wish I could undo it, but I can't. Can you ever forgive me?"

"I… I…don't know. You've disgraced us in front of the whole town and all our friends. Some of these people have only recently begun to like us and trust us and you have made everything worse by what you did."

She was heartbroken as tears welled up in her eyes and slowly rolled down her cheeks splashing onto her lap.

"Maybe my mother was right; you can't trust any white man," she blurted out not really meaning a word of it.

"Lilah, how can you say that? I risked everything for you and your people. I just made a mistake, I'm only human."

"Many people have done cruel things to me in my life, but I never thought you would ever hurt me."

"Lilah, I did not mean to hurt you, I would never deliberately hurt you, and you have to believe me. Besides if you were home, I would never have gotten drunk, I would have been there with you."

"So now it's my fault for trying to help my people and having a job? Am I supposed to just sit home and be a good little wife?"

"That's not what I mean, but I hardly see you anymore and you've changed in your appearance and manner."

"I let my hair grow and I've become a business woman and that gives you the right to cheat on me, with your ex-wife, who still hates me."

"I'm sorry. Tell me what else I can do to make it better."

He got up to hug her; she pushed him away and said, "Don't. Don't touch me."

Delilah reached into her drawer for a cigar, which she lit and puffed incessantly on while she pondered her next move. Jameson kept apologizing and hoping for forgiveness.

Finally she spoke, "Jameson," she never called him Jameson, it was serious, "I want you to leave me alone and go home. I need to think, about us and our future."

"But it was a mistake, Lilah; I would never have done it if I was sober."

"That is your excuse, you were drunk? Would it be okay for me to do the same if I were drunk?"

"Please don't give up on us. I love you. I have always loved you, and I always will love you. I don't want Abigail or any woman, just you."

He looked at her for some sign of forgiveness, but there was none, only tears that he wished he could have wiped away. She again asked him to leave. He reluctantly arose from his chair, kissed her head and walked slowly out the door. He glanced back at his beautiful wife and prayed to God that this was not the end. She seemed to disappear in a cloud of cigar smoke as he got on his horse and rode home, alone.

Upon returning to Serenity, he entered the house and confessed all to Nanny, hoping she would be able to make everything better, as she did when he was a child, but this was different, much more complex.

"Mista Jameson, you have to prove to her that you are sorry, words are not going to do it."

"How do I do that, Nanny?"

"Give her a little time to calm down, then go back into town and bring her home."

"Suppose she won't come?"

"You have to make her, for you and your little child's sake."

Dawnalee heard her father crying and crawled up onto his lap.

"Are you sad, daddy?"

"Yes, honey, Daddy's sad."

"Will I make it better if I kiss you?"

"What, sweetie?"

"Well, when I'm sad, you or mommy always kisses me and it makes me better."

She reached up and gave him a great big kiss on his cheek.

"There, now how do you feel?"

"I feel better, baby, much better, thanks."

He hugged her tightly as a few tears managed to escape out of his eyes and fall on the floor and then disappear into the wooden boards.

She climbed down off his lap and ran off to play. He looked at Nanny.

"You have to go get her and convince her that she is the only woman you love."

He shook his head and decided to do as the wise Nanny said; wait a little while and then go and try to win back his one true love.

He paced back and forth most of the day, wanting to have a drink, but dare not. Every time he heard a horse approach, he ran to the window, praying it was Delilah, but it was not.

It was getting dark and Nanny finally said to him, "Mista Jameson, go get your wife. Make her forgive you and bring her home."

He looked at her, she nodded yes and he ran out the door, harnessed his horse, and raced into town.

Delilah was hard at work in her office, but this time had locked all the doors, in the event that Michelle got it in his mind to pay her a visit once again. She heard a noise in the back room and went to investigate, but found nothing. When she returned to her desk, an unwelcome figure greeted her.

"Hello Mon Amie, did you miss me?"

"Michelle, how did you get in here, all the doors were locked."

"That is true, but I was already in here, in the back room waiting for nightfall so I could surprise you."

Delilah was reaching for her gun, but could not locate it.

"Are you looking for this?" Michelle said as he held up her gun. "I took the liberty of relieving you of it so you could place your undivided attention on me."

"Get out of here or I will scream," Delilah said as she tried to head for the door.

Michelle grabbed her and pulled her close to his body trying to place a kiss upon her lips.

"Your husband is cheating on you, no? And with his ex-wife, tsk, tsk, that is so humiliating. Perhaps you should have an affair also."

She pushed him away and yelled, "Get out!"

Michelle reached into his pocket and produced a gold bracelet.

"Look, I am not such a bad man see; I have bought you a present. Try it on for me, Cheri."

"Where did you get that?"

She took the bauble from his hand and examined it. There was an inscription engraved inside it reading: *To my beloved, Agatha.* Delilah recognized it as one of the items belonging to a citizen of Willow Hills and stolen by Brother Credence.

"Where did you get this? It was stolen, how did you come by it?"

Michelle thought quickly and said, "I found it and thought it would look beautiful on you that is all."

"You didn't think to turn it into your brother and try to find the rightful owner?" She threw the bracelet back at him and repeated her initial order, "Get out of here, now!"

"You refuse a gift from Michelle Le Brute? How dare you."

He became furious and lunged at her. She grabbed a letter opener, threatening, "Come any closer and I will stab you, I swear."

Michelle laughed, drew his sword and with one swish, quickly disarmed her. The weapon fell to the floor. He then placed the sword against her body and with a perfectly placed slice, cut off all the buttons on her blouse allowing the garment to fall open revealing her undergarments. She shrieked and pulled her arms across her chest to hide her figure from the intruder. He laughed again and approached her. She backed up against the wall and realized he had trapped her.

"You would look gorgeous with only those pearls covering your naked body.

A noise came from the front door, Delilah hoped it was her husband, but it was John Stafford. He was again walking the streets at night, as was his custom, because he could not sleep, reliving the horrors of the war he had endured whenever he closed his eyes.

John was cupping his hands over the window to peek inside and he did not like what he saw. He tried the door, it was locked. He placed his sleeve over his hand for protection and pushed his hand through the window breaking the glass. He reached in, unlocked the door and entered.

"Get out of here monsieur."

"Help me John, he's attacking me."

"Let Missus Delilah go, Frenchie."

"Leave now and I will let you live."

"No one hurts Missus Delilah, while I'm around."

"John, be careful, he has a sword."

"I'm not afraid of you, Frenchie."

"You should be, you silly man."

Let Missus Delilah go, I won't let you hurt her."

"I'm not hurting her, just giving her love from a real man."

John Stafford was getting more irate by the second and was losing his temper and his grasp on reality. His face grew red and his eyes began to bulge as he started to inch closer and closer to Michelle. Delilah knew what was coming and tried desperately to intervene.

"John, just go get the sheriff. Run, I'll be alright until you return."

"Yes, run away like the coward you were in the war," Michelle taunted.

"I'll kill you for that."

Michelle was forced to forego his pleasure for the moment and rose to defend himself. He pushed Delilah in back of him and held his sword at attack position.

Delilah switched her persuasive tactics to Michelle, "Are you going to kill an unarmed man?"

"Only if I have to," replied Michelle.

John Stafford again stated his caveat, "Just let Missus Delilah go and no one gets hurt."

"No one but you coward."

"John, be careful, he'll kill you."

John put his arms out and charged at the perpetrator. When he came into range, Michelle wasted no time and lunged forward, John deflected the blade with his arm, receiving a nasty gash in the process. Michelle with a twist of his wrist quickly recovered and managed to strike the soldier again issuing another cut to his other arm. John swung at the Frenchman and hit him in the face as Michelle plunged the blade into the poor soldier's chest. John Stafford was stunned and gasped for air as he slowly fell to the hard cold floor.

Delilah wanted to scream, but was too stunned as Michelle again forced himself on top of her and pushed her to the floor. She tried to slap him but he hit her hard and temporarily dazed her, tearing off the remaining clothes, leaving her exposed and very vulnerable. She pulled her arms across her chest to hide her breasts.

He said, "Don't bother trying to hide them, Cheri, I will see them eventually."

He bashed Delilah back to the floor landing hard on top of her, temporarily knocking the wind out of the frightened lady. He tore at her skirt and ripped it off, loosened his jeans, as she kept squirming trying to free herself and get up. He ripped her panties off and forced himself into her, smiling and telling her to just enjoy it, he was.

At that moment Jameson entered the office, saw the dead body and quickly surmised the situation. He ran and grabbed Michelle, pulling him off of his wife and throwing him against the wall.

"Get off my wife you piece of garbage," Jameson screamed.

Michelle pretended to kneel on the floor where he quickly reached for his sword as Jameson went for his gun. Just as before Michelle showed his agility with the blade and flicked it at Jameson, disarming him and quickly placing the blade directly upon his chest.

"Say goodbye to your husband, Cherie."

"No, don't hurt him!" Delilah demanded as she grabbed for her clothes and quickly wrapped them around herself.

"You coward, you attack a defenseless woman and you sent those rebels to kill me when it was you who murdered their comrade, not me. You only have courage when you have that blade in your hand."

"That is not true, monsieur. I can handle things quite well without it."

"Name me one time you did that."

"I took care of business in the swamp the other day when that crazy woman was trying to kidnap your daughter. I stopped her and I was going to return your little girl to you, but she ran away while I was, uh, tending to other matters."

"You, you killed Bethany Sue?"

I did not say that; don't put words in my mouth. I tried to save your little girl from a deranged woman."

Michelle turned toward Delilah and said, "You see Cherie, I am not such a bad man. I was trying to save your child. Too bad you don't appreciate me more so I wouldn't have to kill your husband."

"Don't. If you hurt him, I'll hate you forever and I swear I'll find a way to kill you myself."

Michelle looked at the hate in her eyes and knew she would never love him, if he hurt her husband. He would have to find another way.

"You are in luck, Hartford; the lady has saved your life again. How does it feel to always have a woman save you? Not much of a man, are you? Honestly Cherie, I don't know how you can love such a weakling. Enjoy your moment; she will not be able to save you ever again."

Michelle started to leave as Delilah ran over to the fallen soldier. Jameson couldn't resist and taunted Michelle a little further hoping the Frenchman would drop his guard and give Jameson the opportunity to enact revenge.

You coward, fight me like a man."

"Stop it James, let him go."

Michelle smirked as he strolled right past the seething Jameson and straight out the door.

Delilah was bent over the dying John Stafford. She grabbed a cloth and tried to stop his bleeding.

"You're going to be alright, John. James, get the doctor."

"Missus Delilah, did I make amends for the hurt I caused you in the past."

"Yes, yes, I forgive you John. You see you're not useless at all, you're a hero."

"Then let me go to my reward. I need to find peace."

"No John, I don't want to lose you. Stay with me, the doctor is coming."

"I'm tired of fighting, Missus Delilah, I want peace."

"John, listen to me, I'll help you; just let me try, ok?"

John Stafford smiled at her and said, "I would do anything for you Missus Delilah, but I can't go on this way, please understand."

Doctor Pritchard arrived but it was too late, the wound was precise in its location and there was no way to save him. The soldier had fought in his last war and sadly had lost this one. He died quietly in Delilah's arms and finally found peace. Delilah wept for the lone soldier and her unlikely friend.

Jameson was confused and said, "I thought you hated him."

"We made up when he saved me from that Brother whatever his name was."

"When did this happen?"

"A while ago, it's not important."

"Nobody told me about that."

"It's in the past."

The argument started up once again as they both went at each other.

The doctor, townspeople and body of John Stafford were removed, leaving the husband and wife alone to settle their differences.

"That's part of our problem. We never talk anymore because I never see you anymore. You're always here working away, day after day and night after night."

"I will never be poor again. Money is power and I will never be under anyone's thumb ever again. Can you understand that?"

"No, I can't."

"That's because you are not black and have never been black and don't know what it is like to be a black. You were rich; no one ever made a slave out of you."

"Delilah, I have never treated you like anything other than my equal. It's true, I can never know what it was like to be persecuted like you and your people were, but I never accepted it and I tried to change it. I gave up my whole life for you."

"And all I'm asking you to do is let me live my life the way I want to live it."

"Does that include me, or just that Frenchman, or maybe you want both of us."

"Get out now, before you say something that you can never take back."

"Well you have to admit, he tells you to grow your hair and you do it."

"I can change my hair if I want to."

"He tells you to wear certain clothes and you wear them."

"I can wear whatever I want."

"I hate that Frenchman, he has to be stopped; I'm going to find him and…"

"Stop it James, not tonight. There is enough death for one day."

"I can handle him."

"That's not it."

"Lilah, if you weren't here working late again, none of this would have happened."

"So it is my fault again, not yours, for adultery? I'll be the laughing stock of the whole town. They'll be pointing at me and saying she can't keep a man, and something must be wrong with her."

"Lilah, none of that is true. It is my fault, not yours. Do you want me to stand on a platform and shout it out to all concerned?"

"It hurts me James. I don't deserve to be hurt, especially by you."

"Delilah, I want you to come home with me, I love you and don't want to fight with you anymore. Please."

Delilah just stared at him, she did not know what to say or do. He turned around and walked out as she broke into tears and sat down at her desk placing her head in her hands, sobbing.

Jameson did not want to go directly home but instead went to look for the elusive Frenchman. He was nowhere to be found. He had crawled into a shadow someplace like the snake he was, waiting to strike again when he felt the time was right. Jameson wound up again at Taffy's. He had a few drinks, perhaps to calm his nerves or maybe to give him courage. Whatever the reason, he was drinking again. Taffy came up to him and told him to go home. Drinking was not going to solve his problems. He knew she was right; he downed the last drop of whiskey in his glass and headed out the door for his horse. Halfway there, he changed his mind and went to see the sheriff about his half-brother. He had had enough of Michelle Le Brute.

Jameson threw open the door to the sheriff's office and demanded that the sheriff keep Michelle away from his wife or he would kill him. Jameson also told him that Michelle killed an unarmed man, who was trying to protect his wife from being raped by the evil half-brother. He also swore Michelle was responsible for murdering Bethany Sue in the swamp, although he could not prove it. Jameson was ranting and raving on and on. Mordechai had never seen him so mad and knew his brother was a dead man if Jameson found him first. He swore he would take care of it as soon as he saw his half-brother again. Jameson told him he had promised to take care of his brother many times before and nothing had changed. This was his last chance. Jameson mounted his horse and started for Serenity, alone.

Mordechai was determined to stop Michelle and arrest him if necessary. This was the last straw and his half-brother had pushed the sheriff to the edge. Mordechai knew what had to be done and he would do whatever was necessary to end the reign of harassment his brother had unleashed on his town. He searched up and down, visiting the favorite haunts of his half-brother, asking everyone he saw of the whereabouts of Michelle, but no one seemed to know a thing. He returned to his office confident that Michelle would turn up there sooner or later, he always did.

# Chapter 17

## *Reminiscing*

Delilah sat in her office feeling alone and betrayed. She was trying to decide whether their marriage was worth saving. Her mind began to travel back as she recalled the first time she met Jameson and how different he was from all other white men she had known up until that time. He was caring and so worried about her and her people. He genuinely wanted to free the poor laborers who worked for him on his plantation and give them a chance at a new life. She recollected how he sacrificed everything; his relatives, family, friends and even his wife, Abigail, so that she, Delilah, would be free. He lost his plantation, his job in Boston and almost all his funds, but never regretted helping her. They fell in love, had a child and he divorced his wife so he could marry her and love her forever. A man has to love you very much to be willing to give up everything for you and try to start over.

She giggled to herself when she recalled how she first met and attended Martha Barrington's School of Etiquette for young women. Those snobbish girls were so nasty to her but Jameson stood by her all the time and she did make the acquaintance of her best friend, Martha.

Then there was that time, during the early years of the Civil War, while they were living in Boston that a knock came upon their door.

Opening the entranceway revealed two people she thought she would never see again, Abigail and Annabelle.

"Hello Nanny, we need to move back home here to Boston as the Yankees are threatening Tall Oaks and we cannot remain there any longer. Please get our bags and have them brought to my room. Thank you ever so much."

Nanny was in shock and did not know what to do. She could not just say no to her former mistress, so she tried to oblige the ladies.

Nanny called to little Dawnalee and said, "Run over to Miss Martha's and get your momma child. Tell her to come back here right now."

Dawnalee dashed across the adjoining lawns to the house next door, yelling, "Mommy, mommy, come quick."

She took her little fist and banged on the large door as best she could. Martha answered the door and glared down on the little girl, who was temporarily frightened.

"Auntie Martha, tell mommy to come home, Nanny needs her."

"What is wrong child?" Martha inquired, as Delilah came running up.

"Sweetie, what is it?"

"There are some strange ladies at our house."

Delilah excused herself, took Dawnalee and headed back to her home. Martha grabbed a sweater to ward off the New England chill and followed.

When Delilah opened the door, she was stunned to find her husband's former wife and her sister. They stared at each other for a brief moment, then Delilah spoke, "What are you doing here?"

"Is that any way to greet visitors, honestly, haven't you learned any manners?" Annabelle said.

"Stop it, Annabelle," Abigail stated, "We've come to live here until the war is over. The Yankees have closed in on Willow Hills and it is not safe. We were hoping Jameson would let us stay here."

Delilah was speechless and did not know how to answer such a request. She certainly did not want either of them in her home but what would her husband say.

"We'll take that as a yes," said Annabelle and again ordered Nanny and the other servants to carry their bags upstairs so they could rest after their treacherous and tiring journey.

"These people are not your slaves and do not take orders from you," Delilah said emphatically.

The tense moment was broken as Martha Barrington entered the house.

"Why hello, Mrs. Barrington, you do remember me don't you, I'm Abigail, Jameson's wife, uh former wife," she said as she glared at Delilah.

Martha was also shocked by the appearance of the two ladies, but in her usual unruffled style, she answered, "Of course I remember you, hello Mrs. uh, what is your last name now dear?"

"It's still Hartford, I never changed it back as I have yet to find another suitable husband," replied Abigail.

"Isn't that curious, we have two Mrs. Hartford's in the same house," remarked Annabelle, as she smirked at Delilah.

"And pray tell who is this little one?"

"This is my, uh, our little girl, Dawnalee."

"Isn't she cute? Hello Honey."

"She is cute. Good thing she looks like Jameson," snickered Annabelle.

Abigail looked around and said, "The house hasn't changed much. Nanny, but where are all my portraits?"

"I had them put into storage in the attic," replied Delilah.

"In heaven's name, why, they were better than these cheap store bought attempts at art you have hung here now."

"I didn't want to look at you all the time," answered Delilah.

"Jealous of the former wife's beauty, are we?" said Annabelle.

Delilah was fuming and everyone could see it, but Annabelle didn't care and continued, "It must be hard to be so… plain. You really should grow your hair and fix your face and at least try to look pretty."

"Stop it, Annabelle," Abigail interrupted, "she can't help it if she is not attractive. Don't make fun of her."

"I want you both out of my house now," demanded Delilah.

"Where are we going to go? You wouldn't just send us back into the midst of the war, would you?"

Again they were interrupted by the hansom cab driver inquiring at the door, "What do you want me to do with these suitcases ma'am?"

"Just bring them in and place them there on the floor, we'll have the help bring it up to our rooms," said Annabelle.

Delilah turned around to see a mound of luggage being brought in and piled up in her living room.

"How many bags are there, six, seven…?"

"There are twelve in total. We only brought the essentials," said Abigail.

Nanny, Delilah and Martha were just standing there in utter disbelief.

"Just show us to our rooms, have our baggage delivered and we'll get out of your hair for a while. Oh I'm sorry, you don't have any hair do you, poor dear," Annabelle said addressing Delilah.

"That won't be necessary, I know my own room," intoned Abigail heading for the stairs.

The two ladies were double teaming poor Delilah and causing her a lot of confusion and anxiety.

She suddenly regained her composure and yelled after Abigail, "Stop, that is my bedroom now and you will not be sleeping in there. It appears we, no you have a problem. This house has only three bedrooms, one belongs to Jameson and I, one is for Nanny and the third is my daughter's. I'm afraid there is no other space available."

"Well Nanny can find someplace else, which frees up one bedroom and…"

"No that is out of the question, Nanny stays in her room. It is hers, she earned it and deserves it and will not be giving it up."

"I can sleep somewhere else Miss Delilah," said Nanny.

"No, Nanny, you will stay in your room, period."

"Then where are we to sleep?"

"Dawnalee can stay with James and I and the two of you can share one room until I discuss this matter with my husband when he gets home from work."

"We have to share one room? How barbaric is that?" cried Annabelle.

"Take it or leave it," demanded Delilah.

"Well, I never, come on Abigail; we'll discuss this with the real master of the house, Jameson when he gets home. He'll straighten her out."

The two sisters paraded upstairs as Delilah called out to them, "You forgot your suitcases. If you want them carry them up yourself."

They ignored her and strutted up the stairs as Nanny showed them the child's room they would be occupying, at least for the moment.

Delilah turned to Martha and said, "Do you believe that? I am so gullible. I should have thrown them out the moment I laid eyes on them. I'm going to go upstairs right now and throw them out on their asses."

"That is not the way a lady speaks, Delilah."

"I don't feel like much of a lady right now."

"Calm down dear, you have to leave it to Jameson; he'll know what to do. If you throw them out, you're the jealous wife; if he throws them out, you're the understanding wife and he's the caring husband."

"That's very devious, Martha."

"I've been around awhile, my dear; I know how to handle a few things."

They both laughed, then Martha said she had to leave, but she stated, "Let me know what happens and if you need me, just call me…ta ta."

Nanny returned from getting the ladies settled and was shaking her head.

"This is a big mess, this is. Those two are trouble, nothing but trouble, mark my words."

"I know Nanny; we'll wait for James and give him the problem."

"Good thinking, Miss Delilah, good thinking."

They went into the kitchen for a nice cup of tea and awaited Jameson's return.

It was 6:00 PM as the front door opened and in walked the unsuspecting Jameson Hartford. Dawnalee ran up to her daddy to get her welcome home kiss as he spotted his wife and Nanny staring at him from the kitchen and an awful lot of suitcases piled up near the door. Delilah came in to welcome him but he could tell there was something amiss, he could feel it in her kiss.

"You're not going to believe who is upstairs."

He could not come close in guessing so she just told him. His mouth dropped open and he asked, "Why?"

Delilah explained and his expression did not change one iota. He just kept shaking his head and saying, "Oh my."

Delilah pressed him for an answer as to what he intended to do about them, but before they could discuss it, down the stairs came the visitors.

"Jameyson, you're home at last," Annabelle said in her sing song baby voice, as she ran and placed her arms around his neck. "You're…wif, er woman was so nasty to me and my sister. You need to speak with her about her manners and her place."

"Hello, Jameson, How are you?" said Abigail.

"Hello Abby,' he said as he pulled Annabelle's arms off from around his neck. "Hello Belle."

"Did you miss us, Jameyson? I missed you. I thought maybe you would be a free man again by now."

"Belle, stop that kind of talk. I don't want to hear you say anything against my wife, do you hear me?"

Annabelle just glossed right over Jameson's comment and continued on her rant.

"Jameyson, she put us both in one room and told us we can't stay here."

Delilah and I will discuss this, but first I think dinner is ready, isn't it Nanny?"

"Yes it is, Mista Jameson."

"Great, let's eat."

"But Jameyson…"

"We will eat in quiet and then discuss this matter, everyone agreed?"

There were no objections so everyone enjoyed a delicious silent meal, but the staring of daggers was apparent to everyone at the table.

When dinner was finished, Jameson and Delilah went up to their bedroom to discuss the matter, alone behind closed doors.

"James, I don't want them here. They were not nice to me. They still think of me and still treat me like I'm their servant."

"I can speak to them about that. Do you want me to send them back to their plantation and the war?"

"I don't know, but I don't want them here. Am I a bad person for wanting them to leave?"

"No, they were wrong for coming here unannounced and thinking they could stay. Let's go speak to them now."

He kissed her and gave her that loving look that told her everything would be alright. She had come to believe that look many times and he had never let her down.

Jameson looked for the two sisters and Nanny told him they were in Dawnalee's bedroom. He and Delilah knocked on the door and entered.

Annabelle again ran up to Jameson and hugged him.

"Did you put her in her place, Jameyson?"

"Belle, I told you not to speak of my wife like that."

"I'm sorry, Jameyson, it's just that I can't see what you like about her."

"Belle, that is enough; get out and leave Abby and us alone."

"But Jameyson…"

"Get out now!" he said so forcefully that Annabelle got scared and quickly departed.

Jameson turned to Abigail who was sitting on the bed and walked over to her.

He sat on the edge of the mattress, took her hand in his, looked into her eyes and said, "Abby, whatever made you come here? You knew how uncomfortable this would be for all concerned, yet the both of you showed up here; unannounced yet."

"Jameson, we were scared and did not know where to go. We are two women living alone on a large plantation in an empty house. The war took all the able bodied men and most of the slaves ran off. When we heard the Yankees were near, we panicked and left. We're alone and frightened. Tell me what to do."

"You can't stay here. I will give you some money and you and your sister can get a room in Boston. Stay there until the war is over and then you can go back home."

Abigail had tears in her eyes as she once again realized Jameson did not belong to her any longer. She had hoped to rekindle a romance that never ended for her, but he was beyond her reach. He was over her and she had lost. She looked at Delilah and apologized for the intrusion and said they would get a coach and leave. Delilah said they could stay for the night and go first thing in the morning. Jameson smiled at his big hearted bride.

That evening, in their room, Jameson told Delilah how nice it was of her to allow Abigail and Annabelle to stay the night. Delilah told him she cares too much; it's a personality flaw of hers. She thanked him for his understanding of her point of view and requesting them to leave, it must have been hard for him. He said surprisingly it was not that hard, because he loved her more than anything.

Delilah then said, "They don't have to be that comfortable, let's make a little noise."

"Oh you are a little mischief maker, aren't you?"

She pulled him in close to her and they proceeded to make some unmistakable sounds causing their next door neighbors a little discomfort; just to insure they would willingly leave the following day.

The next morning the two sisters were on their way. Jameson had called a cab and given them money for a room and some food. He told them to look for employment as there were plenty of jobs in Boston. He would make inquiries for them and help them as much as he could.

After a week had passed, Jameson tried to find them, but they had checked out of the hotel and left him a note:

*Jameson, we are not adapted to northern living and have decided to go back and take our chances in South Carolina. Come visit when you are able, Love Abby and Belle.*

Jameson felt bad but let them go, he never went after them; he was devoted to his wife.


Delilah came back to her senses and after a few minutes, she pulled herself together and decided she did indeed love Jameson and he loved her very much in return. They would have to get over this somehow. She boarded up the broken window pane and headed home to her one true love. She hoped he would be there so she could tell him how much she loved and wanted him and forgave him. They would surmount this obstacle just as they had surmounted all the other obstacles that were put in their path, with love and understanding. She couldn't wait to get home and tell him.

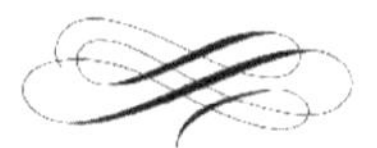

# Chapter 18

## *Reunited*

Delilah arrived at Serenity in her coach and entered the house. She asked Nanny if Jameson was there. Nanny sadly shook her head no. Delilah looked surprised, thought for a moment, then quickly ran up the stairs into her bedroom.

She stood in front of the large mirror and looked at her reflection, she had indeed changed. She decided it was time for another transformation. She reached into the drawer and produced a pair of scissors, then she carefully lifted her hair, a few strands at a time and began to cut them off. She kept cutting her hair shorter and shorter watching each group float to the floor and pile up at her feet. Soon it was too short for her to grasp in her fingers. She placed the scissors down and reached for Jameson's straight razor. She carefully shaved off the stray ends around her ears forming perfect arcs, then straight across the nape of her neck and finally across the front of forehead, shaving a perfectly straight line. She stood there and admired how strong it made her look and how she liked the freedom of short hair. She washed off the excess remnants and towel dried her hair. It was so short it dried in a minute.

She sat down at the vanity and began to apply makeup to her face. She outlined her eyes, daubed powder on her face and applied a red coloring to her lips. A splash of some exotic scented perfume completed the process. Then she took off her clothes and found a very sexy pink negligee and slipped it over her head. It was a little too long so she took the scissors and cut a long slit just left of center and straight up the dress stopping at her waist. She again viewed herself in the mirror and was satisfied with the results. There reflecting back at her was a sexy and alluring nymph, waiting for her lover.

On cue, the front door opened and Jameson entered. He too asked Nanny if his significant other was at home. She smiled and motioned toward the bedroom. He looked and there on the stairs was a goddess in pink. She stood seductively with her leg positioned out of the slit leaving his imagination to run wild. He dropped his hat and coat on the floor and ran to her on the stairs.

"Lilah, you look so beautiful. I'm so happy you're here. I'm so sorry for what happened."

He kissed her passionately and held her in his arms for a long time, not wanting the moment to end.

"Do you like my hair?"

"Lilah, I love it. You would look gorgeous to me if you shaved your head. I'm so in love with you."

"I did it for you, James, I love you. I don't want to fight anymore."

"Me either, I love you so much."

"I'm going to make this a night you'll never forget, James, my love."

"Every night I spend with you is a night I never forget."

He lifted her shapely body into his arms and carried her up the stairs and into their bed. He lay her down on the mattress and quickly undressed, throwing his clothes in all directions. He then climbed on top of her and again kissed her, tasting her, savoring her sweetness. The moment was reminiscent of the very first time they were together, over 5 years ago, sharing a love that was then forbidden for both of them. Times had certainly changed.

He caressed her firmly yet gently in his arms as she sighed in pleasure. She ran her hands down his chest and pulled him in close to her. For a few brief minutes, they would be one in love. They thrust their bodies up and down in unison as if to the beat of a soulful madrigal. Their breathing grew stronger and their bodies grew hotter as she threw him onto his back and took her place on top of him, raising and lowering her body in rhythmic motion, as he beamed with pleasure. The fire was fueled and they could no longer contain the heat. They both moaned as they released their love for each other and for a few seconds nothing mattered but the passion they felt inside for one another. Then she lay on top of him as he held her close not wanting to ever be separated again.

He ran his hands over her short hair and told her how pretty she was and how he loved her in short hair. She smiled and said she would always keep it that way for him. Time seemed to stand still as they looked deep into each other's eyes and saw the reflection of the other so deep in love. They embraced each other in the moment, promising it would last forever.

Jameson then reached into the night stand and produced a cigar and matches.

"Do you remember the first time we shared one of these?"

"Yes, I do."

She grabbed the matches, ignited it and placed the flame to the tip of the cigar in Jameson's mouth. He sucked on the rolled tobacco and then blew the smoke out of his mouth. He handed it to her and she placed it in her lips, took a large puff, forcing her cheeks to indent, she inhaled it deep into her lungs then bent down and placed her open lips on Jameson's mouth, blowing the smoke into his mouth as he inhaled her breath into his lungs. When they parted, he blew her smoke out of his lips.

"We did that too, remember?"

"I could never forget, darling."

They took turns puffing on the cigar as Delilah mused, "James, I've been thinking. I feel we should move back to Boston."

"What, are you serious?"

"Yes, I've done all I can do here. I can turn the businesses over to my employees and you can turn the plantation over to Jeb. We can go back with Dawnalee, Ruby Rose and Nanny and be happy there. I have enough money that we don't even have to work. We can travel; see Europe, maybe Greece or the pyramids in Egypt. What do you think?'

"I think that is a great idea. It's time to worry about us for a change."

"We can start tomorrow, the sooner the better."

"Okay my love."

"Jameson, there is one more thing."

"What darling."

"I think I'm pregnant."

'What, are you sure? Oh that is wonderful news sweetheart. I'm so happy."

"Why didn't you tell me earlier?"

"I was going to, but then you changed the mood with…I don't want to think about that now."

"I agree, but are you sure you're pregnant?"

"I'm having those same old feelings I had before. When we go into town tomorrow, I'll have the doctor confirm it."

"We wanted another child for so long and were not able to conceive one. This is such great news. I wonder what made the difference."

"Maybe it's the water."

He grabbed her and held her so tight; she had to remind him that she could break.

He laughed and said, "I love you so much Lilah," and kissed her right on her newly cropped hair.

"I love you too James."

They finished the cigar, rolled over and held onto each other throughout the night.


Michelle strolled into Mordechai's office as if nothing had happened.

"Where have you been brother?" the sheriff asked.

"Oh, around; here and there; no place special."

"I know what you have been up to and I want you to stop it this instant."

"Whatever do you mean, brother?"

"You've been trying to seduce that Hartford woman again, haven't you?"

"I cannot help it if she finds me attractive."

"Her husband wants to kill you."

"He may want to, but I doubt he can do it."

"Leave her alone."

"I will never leave her alone until I have partaken of her love…and her money."

"You have also killed a number of people: an old soldier, Hartford's sister-in-law, and that corporal that you tried to blame on Hartford. That makes three, I am the sheriff in this town and I have sworn to uphold the law and my own brother is breaking it."

"You are the law. You can make it, interpret it and decide who to arrest and who is innocent."

"Michelle, I have a good thing here and I will not let you ruin it. These people elected me and they can recall me just as fast. I will not stand for your behavior."

"I killed an old soldier that no one wanted and a renegade that no one cared about. I did you a favor brother. Hartford's mother-in-law I will not admit to killing, although nobody really wanted her either; you have no proof of that one, only hearsay evidence."

"They were all people and deserved the same protection under the law as anyone else. You broke the law and I am going to have to arrest you."

"You would arrest your only brother."

"You are only my half-brother and I will uphold the law. You do not have a choice here, you are under arrest. Give me your sword and march yourself into a cell."

Michelle unbuckled his scabbard and as it slipped to the ground he grabbed the sword handle which easily slipped out of its covering, exposing the sharp blade.

He said, "Well then my only half-brother take the steel end of my sword first. See I do have a choice only it is not so good for you."

He plunged the blade deep into Mordechai's abdomen and held it there. The big man looked shocked and teetered on his legs as Michelle guided him backward toward the cells, holding and pushing on the handle of the sword. When he was near a cot, Michelle pushed Mordechai backwards as he pulled the sword out of his body. Mordechai fell on the bed. Michelle cleaned his blade with a nearby blanket and then threw the covering over his brother's dying body, concealing the murder. He then calmly slammed the cell door, walked out of the prisoner's area, shut the door to that area and locked it. He picked up the scabbard, cinched it around his waist and slid the blade back into its resting place.

Michelle then checked the street for passerby's and spying no one, he left the building. He did not see a black cat slide across his path and was startled as the feline glared at him with its glowing green eyes. He jumped back as the cat arched its back and hissed at him, swiping its claw at the stunned Frenchman.

"Get out of here you wretched creature!" he swore at the animal.

The cat just stood there looking at him, seemingly unafraid. He knew what it meant, bad luck and he also remembered where he had seen green eyes like that before, Sapphira. He shuddered, swore at the cat again and proceeded on his way.

Michelle was becoming increasingly unstable and he was about to reach the point of no return.

# Chapter 19

## *Treachery*

That morning they told Nanny the news. She was excited for them and wanted to return to Boston along with her two best friends. Jebediah and Madeline were ecstatic for them, especially about the possibility of another baby. Madeline loved Delilah's haircut and told Jebediah she would like to cut her hair just like that. He could only smile and say whatever you want to do is fine with me. They all were impressed that Jebediah had indeed changed. It was their anniversary and they were going into town later to celebrate with a dinner at the restaurant and would be home late.

Delilah and Jameson entered the town of Willow Hills, each with their own list of things to accomplish. The whole town witnessed them riding together and acting very much in love dispelling any rumors of scandal and divorce.

Annabelle and Abigail were in town also and witnessed the affection.

Anabelle said, "That is horrible. He gets you pregnant and flaunts it with that, that woman."

"You mean his wife? Forget it Annabelle. He belongs to her and that is the end of it."

"That is not the end of it. I won't have it."

What do you mean?"

"Nothing, just wait here."

Annabelle strolled off, looking for her evil accomplice, Michelle. Abigail, being suspicious, followed close behind.

Delilah called all her employees together and made the announcement that she will be leaving and turning the businesses over to them. They were shocked but wished her the best and continually thanked her for all she had done. They insisted upon a party to thank her and her husband for all they had done for the community. It would be a gala the entire town would celebrate. She reluctantly agreed, but said they had to do it soon as Jameson and her wanted to leave for Boston as quickly as possible.

Jameson went to the bank to have all the papers drawn up to turn the plantation over to Jebediah and Madeline. Everyone was shocked and the news spread fast throughout the growing town. It soon made its way to Taffeta Jones Gentleman's Emporium and to one customer in particular who was already inebriated, Michelle Le Brute.

He grabbed the messenger, who delivered the news and questioned him at length, finally releasing him when he was satisfied that it was true. He walked out onto the street and met up with Anabelle, who pushed him into an alley off the main thoroughfare. There she confronted him.

"Did you hear the news?"

"Yes, I have heard it."

"You failed. I thought I could rely on you to break them up, but you couldn't do it. You with all your high-falootin' talk and rants, you are just a lot of hot air."

"Shut up you little snake."

"Don't tell me to shut up. We had a deal. You seduce that woman and I get Jameson."

"You mean he doesn't want your sister even after he got her pregnant?"

"No."

"Well that is too bad, but I still want the money you promised me."

"What? You didn't live up to your side of the bargain. The deal is off."

"No, I need the money. You don't understand."

"Too bad."

He grabbed her arm, at which point she said, "Let me go or I'll scream."

Michelle was ready to silence her when his eyes caught someone watching them intently. He knew he could not afford a scene, especially with a witness, so he let her go but said, "This is not over."

He walked away down the alley. Annabelle turned around and was surprised to find Abigail standing there.

"What did you do Annabelle?"

"Nothing, I don't know what you are talking about."

"Annabelle, I saw you talking to that Frenchman and I heard something about seducing Delilah so you could have Jameson. Now what did you do?"

At first Annabelle claimed innocence, but upon further cross examination, she confessed all.

"Alright, alright, I tried to get him to seduce that woman so Jameson would leave her and be with us, I mean you. That's all."

"Call it off now, Anabelle. That man is unbalanced and if you don't, I'll tell Jameson the whole sordid story."

"No, you'll ruin everything if you do that."

"I'm not fooling around, stop it now!"

"Okay, okay, let me go find him."

Anabelle walked off but could not locate the elusive Michelle. When she met up with her sister, she lied and said she took care of it. Abigail believed her and went to the doctor's office for a checkup. Anabelle went home to Tall Oaks.

Abigail entered Doctor Pritchard's office and was met face to face with Delilah. The two stared at each other, Doc just sighed, "I think I'm having a Deja vu moment."

Abigail began, "What are you doing here?"

"Doctor, what am I doing here?"

"Well Delilah, you are indeed pregnant, congratulations!"

"You're pregnant too?"

"Yes, how about that? We're both pregnant at the same time by the same man. Talk about coincidences."

"I always wanted a child and now my dream has come true and with the man I love."

"He doesn't love you, at least not anymore."

"How do you know? How can you be so sure? Maybe you lost him to me just like I lost him to you those many years ago."

"I would never want to lose him."

"Well if I know Jameson he will never leave his child so he will always be spending time with me."

Delilah had never thought of that and she suddenly became quiet as tears welled up in her eyes. She supposed he would never leave a child he had fathered and would always have that connection to Abigail; would they be returning to Boston or not? But the quick thinking and feisty woman would not be outdone and fired back, "James will always stay with me, our two daughters and soon to be family of three. He will never leave us for you."

Abigail hesitated; ready to ignite the smoldering fire then suddenly changed her demeanor and said, "I don't want to be like this anymore. You know he was drunk that night. He did not know what he was doing. He loves you."

"Being inebriated is no excuse for anything, however he did apologize and he is sorry and I do love him, so I have forgiven him. Besides, we are planning to go back to Boston."

"I know I heard the news; I guess I was hoping that the baby would… well never mind. You have him; don't lose him like I did. I was foolish."

Delilah felt a little sorry for her one time adversary.

"He will help you monetarily with the child. You won't be poor."

"I'll only be alone and heartbroken," Abigail said as she began to cry.

Again Delilah felt sorrow for the former wife and somehow the words came out of her mouth, "You are welcome to visit us whenever you want. I don't want you or James's child to be alone. Besides I'm sure he would like to see the child."

"That would be okay with you? You are a better person than I am. I can see why he loves you. You have a big heart."

"Thank you…Abigail."

"You're welcome…Delilah."

That was the first time they had ever addressed each other by their God given names, and it seemed that perhaps maybe they could be friends, or at least friendly toward each other. They briefly embraced and then Delilah left the office found Jameson and told him of her encounter with Abigail. She told him she was indeed pregnant and he was ecstatic, kissing her and smiling uncontrollably. She said the doctor wanted her to rest due to the fact of her previous miscarriages, so she decided to go home. He said he had to wait for the papers to be drawn up then he would follow her. He would borrow a horse in town and be home shortly. They parted company, as she left in her coach.

Annabelle arrived at Tall Oaks and was so upset over the day's events that she decided to fix herself a drink, wondering why the house was so dark. She took the drink and went upstairs to her room. She removed her dress and was startled by the figure of a man standing there looking at her.

She recognized him and yelled, "Michelle Le Brute, get out of my house."

"I want the money you promised me."

"You didn't earn it. The deal was for you to break up Jameson and his…wife. You couldn't even seduce a Negro girl. What kind of man are you?"

His face reddened and his voice grew louder.

"You do not know what you are talking about. I need the money, now."

There was something evil in his eyes and Annabelle became frightened.

"Alright, I'll get it for you. It's right over here in the drawer."

Anabelle reached in and pulled out a pistol. She was no match for the quick reflexes of the master swordsman. He disarmed her rather easily, then attacked her, ripping off her clothes and forcing himself upon her. She tried to resist but he kept hitting her first with his open hand and then with closed fists; all the time he was enjoying her body. She started screaming then the sounds turned to barely audible whimpers, as she became closer and closer to unconsciousness. When he was finished, he pulled up his trousers and ransacked her room searching for the money he felt he was owed, while the lifeless body of Annabelle lay strewn across the bed.


Abigail returned home and found the house strangely quiet.

"Annabelle, are you home? Where is everyone?"

She climbed the stairs and headed for Annabelle's room, calling out, "Are you there Anabelle? Where could you be?"

Abigail entered her sister's room and saw Annabelle's body on the bed. She rushed over to it and felt for a pulse; Annabelle moaned. Then she noticed how black and blue her sister's face was. Someone had beaten her badly; she turned to run for help but was stopped by an irrational figure coming out of the shadows.

"Going someplace Mon Cheri?"

Abigail was shocked to see the Frenchman standing there.

"What, what are you doing here?'

"I came to collect the money your sister owed me, but she was not cooperative. I tried to persuade her, I guess I tried too hard."

"I, I have to leave."

"Oh no Mon Amie, I can't let you do that. You would tell on me, would you not?"

"Let me go, please let me go. I'm with child."

"I know, Hartford's bastard child.  I hate him too, maybe as much as you, no? I'm going to get his wife when I leave here. I will finally have her."

Abigail was shaking but managed to speak, "What are you going to do to me?"

"I have no choice, I have to silence you."

Abigail screamed, pushed him aside and tried to run, but he was too strong for her. He grabbed her and pulled her back. She took her finger nails and scratched his face. He loosened his grip and she tried to flee once more.

She only got a few steps away as he again took hold of her and pulled her back into her bedroom. She screamed and kicked, desperately trying to escape, as Annabelle was moaning and crying in the adjoining room, wanting desperately to help her older sister.

He hit Abigail and said, 'Please be quiet. It is such a pity to have to kill someone so pretty. Don't make it worse with all that screaming."

Abigail once more scratched him but this time went for the eyes.

He screamed, "Damn you, you little wench, you are not worth the trouble."

She again broke free and tried to run but the point of a blade stopped her in her tracks. She fell to the floor whimpering as a demented Michelle continued to search the room for money. He found jewels and figured they would have to suffice. He stepped over the bleeding body of Abigail and headed out the door, straight for Serenity.


Jameson was ready to leave town but decided to revisit the sheriff and find out if he heard from his brother. Jameson wanted to verify the whereabouts of Michelle and be assured he would not bother his wife any longer.

He was stopped by Doctor Pritchard who asked him, "Jameson, could you return this purse to Abigail on your way back to Serenity? She left it in my office today after her exam. She was there at the same time as Delilah."

"I bet that was awkward. They didn't fight again, did they?"

"They were actually very civil to each other. I'm sure you'll hear all the details from Delilah."

"I'm sure I will."

"Jameson, sorry to hear you will be leaving. This town really needed the both of you. Will I see you again before you leave?"

"Yes, doctor, I'll be sure to stop and say goodbye to you."

The two old friends nodded and smiled at each other as Jameson reluctantly accepted the purse. He didn't really want to see Abigail alone but figured he should probably say something to her about their baby and his leaving to return to Boston. *Maybe I will deliver it tomorrow when I'm with Delilah*, he thought as he headed for the sheriff's office.

He was surprised to find the office vacant. He tried the door to the cell area and found it locked. He could see through the little window that someone was in one of the cells. He assumed it was Michelle and wanted to be sure. Jameson found the keys and opened the outer door. He approached the cell and saw a pool of blood on the floor under the cot. He could not identify the occupant as they had a blanket over them. He opened the cell door and approached the bed. He threw back the blanket and there was the lifeless body of Mordechai Le Brute, the sheriff.

Shocked for a second, Jameson stood there, then judging from the cut, ascertained it was a puncture wound from a sword, he thought: *Michelle must have done this*. He ran out of the office, grabbed the nearest person and told him what happened. He thought again and told the citizen to go to the restaurant and tell Jebediah and Madeline what happened and to get back to Serenity fast. With that, Jameson hopped on his horse and galloped for home.


Jameson was passing Tall Oaks and still debating with himself as to whether he should return the purse today or tomorrow, when a little voice inside his head told him to stop and check on Abigail. He did not know why but he obeyed his instinct. The door was partially ajar and he now knew something must be wrong. He entered and looked around.

It was dark and quiet. He heard a soft moan coming from the upstairs rooms.

He quickly ran up the stairs and into the first room. Annabelle was still lying helpless across the bed. She was badly beaten but was still alive. He ran up to her.

"Belle, can you hear me? Are you alright? What happened?"

She opened her eyes and could barely make out the figure of the man she had desperately wanted for so long.

She mumbled, Jameyson, Is that you? You came to save me."

He told her everything would be alright and asked where Abigail was. She mumbled something, when he heard another moan coming from another bedroom. He told her he would be right back and ran to find Abigail lying on the floor in a puddle of blood.

"Oh my God, Abby, what happened? Who did this to you?"

She looked up at her knight in shining armor and whispered, "Michelle, he did this to us."

Jameson said, "Don't worry; I'll get you into town to the doctor. You'll be safe."

She struggled to speak, and finally managed to say, "He is going after Delilah. You have to save her. Forget me, save your wife and baby."

Panic spread across Jameson's whole body as he realized the dilemma he was facing; does he save his former wife and baby or the woman he loved and their baby. He hesitated to ponder the situation, as Abigail urged him to go. He could not let the two of them die and had to try to save everyone. He only hoped he could perform such a miracle.

He tried to stop Abigail's bleeding by stuffing bits of loose fabric into the gaping wound holes, and then scooped her up in his arms and carried her down to her coach, placing her gently in the back. He then ran back for Annabelle and did the same for her, telling them to hold onto each other for stability as he had to get them back into town as quickly as possible. They agreed as he hit the horses with the reins and off they went.

Scarcely making it to the main road, he stumbled upon Jebediah and Madeline, who were coming back from town, per Jameson's instructions. He told them to take the women back into town to the doctor and then hurry back to Serenity as Michelle was going there to hurt Delilah. They agreed and Jameson was once again heading to Serenity to save his wife.

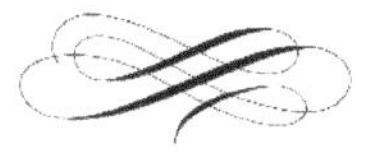

# Chapter 20

## *Abduction*

The air was hot and sticky, typical for a South Carolina summer, so the breeze felt good as it blew past the determined rider. Sunlight flickered on and off through the passing trees as Jameson kept the horse at a gallop, hoping to get to Serenity as fast as possible.

Michelle had arrived at the plantation and burst through the door. Nanny was in the kitchen cooking and Dawnalee and Ruby Rose were helping her.

Nanny boldly told him, "Get out of here. Who do you think you are walking right into a person's home without being invited? You ain't no gentleman."

Michelle paid no attention to her but called out for Delilah. She had been resting in her room as the doctor ordered and wondered what all the yelling was about. She recognized the voice and accent and knew he meant to harm her. She took a loaded pistol from the nightstand, hid it on her person and proceeded down the stairs.

"There you are Mon Cherie. You knew I would come for you, no?"

"Get out of my house, now!"

"I told him to leave Miss Delilah, but he wouldn't listen."

Delilah pulled out her gun and pointed it at the Frenchman, again telling him to leave.

He was no fool and said, "Alright, my love, if that is really the way you want it, I will go," and turned to leave but instead made a dash for the kitchen and grabbed Dawnalee.

"Now who is holding the winning hand in our little game, huh?"

"Don't hurt her, Let her go."

"Then drop the gun and come down here now."

Ruby Rose ran up to the man and started hitting him on the legs saying, "Let my sister go."

Michelle pushed the child away and told Nanny to keep the child away from him or he would hurt her.

Delilah had no choice but to comply with the demand. She dropped the gun and proceeded down the stairs.

"Come closer my love," he ordered.

She approached him, "Let go of my little girl."

"As soon as you are in my grasp."

Then his pleasant demeanor turned ugly as he noticed she had cut her hair short.

"Why did you cut off all your hair? I told you to grow it long. I don't like it at all. I am very upset with you."

Delilah tried to calm him down as there was no telling what he was capable of doing in this state. Besides, she had to stall until Jameson came home. He should be there any minute.

"I'm sorry, but it will grow back."

"I have to punish you for disobeying me. Cherie."

He still had Dawnalee in his grasp and was going to get even with Delilah by hurting her child.

"No, don't you touch my child," she screamed.

Nanny grabbed a frying pan and charged the Frenchman in an effort to save the child. He was forced to let go of Dawnalee and protect himself by hitting the poor older woman sending her to the hard wood floor, with a thump.

Ruby Rose started kicking him and as he tried to backhand the child, she bit him forcing swear words out of his mouth. He warned Delilah of the consequences if this kept up. Delilah told Ruby Rose to go and help Nanny.

Nanny was still lying on the floor complaining, "Oh my back," and could not seem to get up.

Delilah tried to escape but was snared by Michelle.

"Not so fast, you are mine now," he stated as he pulled her close to him and tried to kiss her.

She fought back and kept turning her head so he could not connect with her lips. He was getting angrier and told her if she did not go along with him willingly he would take the child instead. Delilah tried to talk to him and calm him down.

"Please, you don't understand I'm married; I can't cheat on my husband. If I were single, there is no man I would rather be with than you. You are handsome; so virile, and that accent, what girl could resist that French accent."

He relished the compliments and was enjoying the moment. She was stalling for time, wondering where Jameson was and when he would return. In the meantime, it was up to her to save them.

"Can you wait until I get a divorce from James, then we can be together and I would not be committing a sin?"

He looked at her and said, "I don't want to marry you. Michelle is not the marrying kind. I just want to have some fun with you. I don't care if it is a sin or not. I'm going to hell anyway, might as well enjoy myself until then."

He laughed and again forced himself upon her, telling her to come with him or he would hurt the child.

Delilah knew he was not fooling and turned to Dawnlee. She told the child to go with Ruby Rose and hide in their secret spot. The children took off as Michelle tried to go after them but was detained by Delilah who grabbed his face and gave him a great big kiss. His male ego could not resist and he temporarily forgot the children.

The secret spot was the passageway from the closet to the barn. Dawnalee and Ruby Rose obeyed their mother and ran for the door disappearing in a second.

Feeling he was once again made to look the fool, Michelle grabbed Delilah and told her to come with him or he would kill Nanny. She reluctantly agreed and he led her away by the arm out the door.

In the distance he could see a horse and a rider which he assumed was Jameson. He panicked, knowing two people on one horse could not out run a single rider so instead, he grabbed his rope, tied it around Delilah's waist and dragged his prize into the woods and toward the swamp. He told her to be quiet or he would silence her.

"If I can't have you, nobody will have you."

She knew what he was capable of so she did not make a sound. Besides she had to think of her unborn child.

Delilah moved very slow pushing the brush and limbs away from her, turning to the left and then to the right in an attempt to slow their progress telling her captor she did not know where she was going. Michelle decided to take the lead and went ahead of her pulling her along as he trudged through the woods.

Delilah knew Jameson would never be able to find her so somehow she had to mark their path. She thought for a second, and then an ingenious idea occurred to her. She tugged at her pearl necklace until it broke. She gathered the pearls in her hand and began to drop them one at a time at specific intervals in an attempt to mark her trail. Michelle was too busy navigating through the swamp to notice anything and she had secured a way for Jameson to be able to follow her.

Jameson rode up to the plantation and spied a strange horse tied up at the front porch. He surmised Michelle was inside and pulled out his pistol. Dawnalee and Ruby rose came running out of the barn where the passage had led them and yelled for their father.

"Daddy, daddy, the man with the funny voice from the swamp took mommy."

"Are you alright, my babies?"

"Yes, daddy but mommy is gone."

"Where did they go?"

"Here, daddy, I'll show you."

The little girl ran toward the forest.

"No, Dawnalee, stay here, daddy will go after mommy."

"Nanny is hurt too, daddy."

Marcus and Ambrosia came running up to the house from the fields.

"What is going on Jameson?"

That Frenchman has kidnapped Delilah and taken her into the forest, no doubt directly into the swamp. I'm going after her."

"We'll go with you."

"Ambrosia, stay here and take care of Dawnalee and Ruby Rose and see what happened to Nanny; she is hurt in the house. Then get some more men out of the fields to come and help me. Marcus, you come with me now, I need you."

"I'm with you, Jameson. Don't worry, we'll find her."

The two men ran off into the forest and into the swamp. Not knowing what direction they would take or if they would even find their way back out, but they had to find Delilah before the madman Michelle did anything to her.

# Chapter 21

## *Pursuit*

The trees quickly closed in upon them and the sunlight faded away, hidden by the lush thick forestation. The air was heavy and you could smell the moisture, as it smothered you with its stench.

"Where do we go?" Marcus asked.

"I don't know. I guess we'll have to split up. We can cover more ground that way."

Marcus spied something shiny on the ground. He bent down to pick it up, looked carefully at it, then called to Jameson.

"Look at this! Isn't this one of Delilah's pearls?"

Jameson took the small round ball, held it up to the light and watched it magically capture the light and mysteriously glow. He knew it was Delilah's pearl.

"Look, there's another one."

Marcus bent over and found the second pearl.

"She must be leavin' us a path to follow."

"I think you're right. Let's keep going in this direction. Look another one."

The pearls were glistening like small moons in the vast wasteland, lighting the way for the rescuers. They were so excited; they rushed headlong into the swamp with little regard to where they were going.

Suddenly the ground gave way beneath Marcus and he began to descend. He had inadvertently stepped into quicksand and was sinking fast.

"Jameson, help me," he shouted.

Jameson stopped and turned around to find Marcus up to his waist in the ooze. Marcus was thrashing around and disturbing the marsh. Once again Jameson was faced with a decision: save his wife or help his friend. He again hoped he could succeed at both and ran to Marcus's assistance.

"Don't move, it will make you sink faster, be still, I'm coming."

Marcus felt something next to him and instinctively grabbed onto it and pulled on it. Suddenly, the body of a man bobbed to the surface, right next to him, with an eerie look on his face. Both of his eyes and his mouth were wide open as if he was screaming at Marcus for help. He shrieked and jumped around all the more, causing another body to float up next to him on the other side. This one was, Brother Credence. Marcus was now surrounded by two bodies seeming to grab hold of him and drag him down right along with them. He shrieked and pushed at the bodies all the faster sinking into the morass.

Jameson grabbed a large branch from the forest floor and held it out to Marcus yelling, "Grab onto it and I'll try to pull you out."

Marcus was trying to reach for it, but it was just out of his grasp and he was now up to his chin in the quicksand.

Jameson leaned in as far as he could without falling into the muck and said, "Grab it, Marcus, please grab it."

Marcus gave it one last attempt and managed to get a hold. Now it was Jameson's turn to tow his friend to safety. He tugged and pulled and carefully backed up but the branch would not hold and cracked in two. Both men went backward; Jameson onto the solid ground and Marcus deeper into the liquid sludge. This time a third body bobbed up along with the other two, a woman with unnervingly green eyes staring at the trapped man. It was the gypsy woman, Sapphira who had disappeared from Willow Hills a few months earlier. One after the other they seemed to grab at Marcus trying to take another soul down with them to the hellish depths of the swamp. He fought them off as he panicked all the more and screamed at Jameson for help.

Michelle and Delilah could hear the screams in the distance.

Michelle laughed and said, "Looks like no one will be coming to save you, Cheri."

"How do you know where you are going? Everything looks the same. We will get lost in here."

"Relax, Mon Cheri, I am very familiar with swamps and bayous from my days in New Orleans. I have had to navigate through much worse than this when I was trying to elude capture from my time as a thief stealing gold and silver from rich aristocrats. It was not legal but I made a very good living. I lost most of it on gambling, fine food, expensive wine and wild women. I now need a rich woman such as yourself to keep me in the manner of living to which I have become accustomed."

Delilah seeing Michelle lost in the moment took the opportunity to scream for Jameson. He grabbed her, put his hand over her mouth and again warned her to be quiet or he would be forced to hurt her. She obeyed if only for her unborn child.

Jameson could not hear his bride's scream as he was frantically searching the area for something to pull his friend out of the muck. There hanging from a nearby tree was a length of rope.

"*That's odd,*" thought Jameson, "*I did not see that before.*"

He picked up the rope and threw one end of it to the drowning Marcus who was almost up to his eyes. He only had one chance at this so he had better be accurate with his throw. He was. Marcus grabbed the rope and Jameson steadied himself on the shore and pulled on the rope. Slowly but surely Marcus came ashore onto solid ground. He stood up and looked at his body and clothes which were covered with the gooey mess and again thanked Jameson for saving his life. The two smiled at each other and breathed a heavy sigh.

"So that's where he hid the bodies, in the swamp; very clever. If it wasn't for you, no one would have ever found those two bodies."

"I wish I hadn't."

"C'mon, we have to get going. He has a bigger lead now."

Marcus shook himself off and the two men were again in search of the elusive pearls, but were a little more careful as to where they stepped.

# Chapter 22

## *Finales*

Michelle had taken Delilah deep into the swamp and she was almost out of pearls.

She asked, "Where are we going?"

"We are going through the swamp, and out the other side, into Georgia, Alabama, Mississippi, and finally back to New Orleans, where we will live together. You will have your riches delivered to the bank there. We will live happily ever after, doesn't that sound like fun?"

"Yes, yes, it certainly does, Michelle," Delilah lied.

"I had treasure buried around here."

He searched but found only a large hole. His ill-gotten gains were gone.

"Someone has stolen my wealth. They will pay for this."

He was furious and was getting more and more delusional as they pushed on through the muck and mire. There was a clearing ahead, which Delilah hoped was their destination as she was growing very tired. Then out of the steamy mist emerged before them a cabin.

"Ah, my home away from home; I have hid out many times in this shack until, as you say, the coast was clear and the furor had died down."

Delilah dropped her last pearl and prayed that Jameson was near and would find her.

As they entered, they were surprised by an eerie figure in a robe with long hair and large scary eyes. Was it the so called "swamp monster," no it was Bethany Sue.

"What are you doing in my home? Get out!"

Delilah was scared, Michelle was not and answered back, "you…the crazy lady, this is your cabin?"

"I am not crazy," she screamed, "Why does everybody keep saying that?"

Bethany Sue had escaped from the mental hospital and returned to her one time home, Serenity. With no one there and no place else to go, she retired into the swamp to live a lonely existence with nature and the creatures of the wetland as her friends. She found an abandoned cabin and made it her own using the skins of dead animals for warmth and robbing from the local farms and businesses for supplemental food and water. Sneaking around in shabby clothes making wild noises and only being seen at night, a local legend grew around her. The folktale of the swamp monster; there is always some truth to every fairytale.

Did you steal my treasure? You saw me hide it there and you dug it up and took it, didn't you?"

"I did not take it. I have no use for it. You are a bad person and I will not let you hurt this woman as you did those others."

"What are you talking about? You know nothing."

"I saw you kill that big man and then try to kill me only my niece stopped you. You chased after her but she got away, back to her home. If you tried to hurt her I would have killed you."

"You, you saved my baby," Delilah said to Bethany Sue.

"No one will ever hurt my niece."

Delilah was sure Bethany Sue was still delirious and did not know who she was as she hated Delilah and had herself tried to kill her on several occasions. She certainly wouldn't try to save her now unless… Dawnalee had managed to soften her heart.

"This is all so sentimental. I am touched. Too bad neither one of you will be able to tell anybody," Michelle bragged.

Bethany Sue looked menacingly at him and said again, "I will not let you hurt anyone else. I left a rope for the men following you and they will soon be here, now leave the lady with me and get out of my swamp, or I will kill you."

"No, my irrational friend, that is not how this will end; I will kill you."

And with that, Michelle drew his sword and lunged at the woman. She shrieked and averted the first strike and sidestepped the second, but Michelle was unrelenting. As he went on the attack, the old woman screeched and started to throw, plates, utensils and anything else she could get her hands on at the intruder. Michelle with his master swordsmanship managed to deflect every incoming object.

Bethany Sue then lifted the pot of stew off the fire and flung it at Michelle. Liquid was the one thing he could not repel and even though he tried to dodge it, the hot fluid managed to find its mark.

Michelle was furious, cursed at the old woman and again went on the attack. Bethany Sue grabbed for a rabbit pelt and tried to grab the blade. It was too sharp and split the hide and then sliced through her hand. She recoiled in pain and Michelle saw his opportunity. He took his saber and plunged it deep into Bethany Sue's chest. She was undaunted or perhaps impervious to the pain and was determined to have her revenge. She lunged at her assailant using her long nails to scratch deep gashes into the Frenchman's face as they fell backward onto the floor. He was temporarily blinded by the blood and the stench of the woman took his breath away. They both gasped for air as the wound in Bethany Sue's chest took its toll and she grew weaker and invariably succumbed to her wound. She lay dormant on top of the Frenchman pinning him under her dead weight.

It was ironic that Bethany Sue had once wanted Delilah dead and was now her only salvation.

Delilah saw this as an opportunity to escape and slowly crept backward and then turned and ran. To hide her escape route she decided to run through the stagnant water. It was deeper than she imagined and as she waded through, she noticed something slithering through the quiet dark water. It was an alligator and it was gaining on her. She tried to propel her legs to move faster but the water would not allow it. She managed to get onto the shore and fell forward, crawling away as fast as she could. The reptile was not too cheated of his dinner and followed her at a rapid pace. She kept pushing herself backwards with her legs until she reached a tree and could not go any further. The reptile gained on her and opened its huge mouth to reveal rows of razor sharp teeth. She thought this was the end when a steel blade was suddenly thrust through the creature's head and it sunk backwards into the water.

Michelle stood over her and said, "You were trying to escape. I am disappointed in you. This calls for punishment so you will not do it again."

Delilah thought quickly and said, "No, no I was afraid that is all."

Michelle almost believed her when he noticed that her pearl necklace was gone and he grew suspicious.

"Where are your pearls?"

"My pearls? Delilah felt her neck. "I…I don't know, I must have lost it in the swamp."

"You think you can fool me, Cherie? Huh… well you can't. You thought you would leave a trail for your husband, huh?  I am most disappointed in you." He dragged her back into the cabin and tied her to a large wooden support post.

"I will have to teach you a lesson. No one lies to Michelle Le Brute."

He bent down, looked squarely into her eyes and then slapped her directly in the face.

"Go ahead and scream no one will hear you except the alligators."

He laughed and hit her again.

"Have you learned your lesson yet?" he taunted her as he bent down to kiss her. She spit directly in his eyes.

He cursed and hit her harder, then closed his fist and said, "This will soften you up. Perhaps a few blows to the stomach will change your mind; I do not want to scar such a beautiful face."

"No, no, not the stomach, I'm pregnant," Delilah yelled.

She had no alternative but to tell the Frenchman, perhaps he would have a little pity on her.

"Is it mine?" he queried.

She was silent, hoping not to antagonize him any further.

"It is Hartford's, isn't it?"

She was frightened for herself and her child.

"What should I care if I hurt Hartford's baby?"

"Please, please, don't hurt my baby," she begged.

Delilah screamed as he made a fist and pulled his arm back to gain momentum.

A voice came from the outside, "Lilah are you in there? Are you alright?"

Jameson's voice stopped the punishment as Michelle knew he had been found. He was both mad and disappointed at this sudden turn of events. He had underestimated his adversary and wasted too much time, now he would have to face Jameson one more time.

Delilah screamed, "I'm here James. I'm alright."

Michelle yelled, "Do not come in here, Hartford or I will kill her and neither one of us will have her."

"What do you want, Michelle?"

"I want you to leave and let me have her."

"That's not going to happen."

"You have no choice in the matter. If you stay here, I will kill you. I suggest you run for your life and let me enjoy this beautiful creature and let her enjoy a real man."

Jameson told Marcus to stay hidden and try to work his way around to the back of the cabin without being noticed. He would try to lure Michelle out and give Marcus a chance to go in and save Delilah.

Jameson called out, "If you are a real man, you will come out and face me so we can settle this once and for all."

Michelle looked out of the cabin checked the surroundings and could not see anyone else.

"You have come alone, monsieur?"

"I'm standing here all by myself aren't I?"

Michelle walked outside and looked at Jameson. For a few seconds, all you could hear was the sounds of the crickets and nocturnal creatures calling to each other. The air was thick and moist with the smell of rotting wood and plants. Michelle and Jameson walked toward each other.

Delilah was trying to free herself by working her arms up and down along the wooden pole, causing the rope to shred. It was coming apart slowly but surely.

"Let's settle this like men, using our fists."

"No, Jameson, you challenged me to this duel; therefore I have choice of weapons, and I choose sabers."

"I don't have a sword."

"That is most unfortunate for you."

Michelle pulled his sword from its scabbard and yelled, "En gard!"

Jameson backed up, out of reach of the blade.

"For a man who claims he is a gentleman, this is not fair at all. It goes against all the rules of a proper duel."

"Who is going to tell on me? You will be dead."

"Michelle, all I want is my wife. Give her back to me and I will leave. You can go your own way."

"I do not want only your wife monsieur, I want her money also. Once I get her money, you can have her back, a little more worn perhaps, but still in good condition."

"You can have the money, just give me Delilah."

"Once I give her to you, you will not live up to your side of the bargain."

"Yes, I will. You have my word on it."

"You're word, hah; I don't keep my word, why would I believe you? No, it has to be this way."

Jameson reached for his pistol and aimed it at Michelle. The master swordsman lunged at his foe as the gun went off. Michelle was not as lucky this time and suffered a wound to the shoulder. He managed to disarm Jameson before dropping his sword and grabbing at the wound.

Delilah had succeeded in freeing herself and ran out the door screaming, "James, James."

Jameson saw his beautiful wife and his instinct to save her kicked in as he ran toward her. Michelle quickly picked up the blade and plunged it deep into Jameson as he ran past him. Jameson continued in his forward momentum and it carried him directly into Delilah's arms. He looked at her in disbelief.

She screamed, "You stabbed him."

Michelle dropped his sword in an attempt to wrap a tourniquet around his bullet wound and stop the bleeding. Delilah momentarily left Jameson, picked up the blade and pushed it right into Michelle's back until it came out through his abdomen.

He was startled and said, "Cherie, cetait toi, what have you done?"

Michelle stumbled off wobbling on his feet, trying desperately to grab the sword in his back that was just out of his reach, all the while recalling the gypsy lady's curse: that he would die by his own sword with a wound inflicted by someone he loved. He teetered, lost his footing and fell by the swamp water. The normally still dark water rippled with action as a large alligator arose, opened its huge jaws and bit hard into the Frenchman's body. He screamed in agony and begged for help as the gator closed its mouth. You could hear the bones crunch. The alligator then death rolled over and over again and took its prize under the water. After a few bubbles, the water became calm once again.

Marcus arrived on the scene and Delilah said, "He's bleeding badly, we have to stop it."

She ripped a bit of her undergarment and tied it tight around Jameson's body hoping to stem the flow of blood.

"We have to get him out of here, now."

Marcus lifted his limp body and said, "Let me carry him. Let's go."

But which way was out. They were confused and turned around. The swamp looked the same in all directions.

"Where do I go, Delilah?"

"I don't know for sure, but let's try to find and follow the pearls I dropped. I think I came from that direction."

She pointed north and they began the search for the elusive pearls. They found the first bead then started to run in that direction, following the glistening balls of light. However, they were not always easy to find in the mud and muck.

Marcus was a strong man and could handle large bundles, but Jameson was fading and a limp lifeless body was heavier and harder to carry. Besides that, they had to watch out for quicksand, and were hoping to reach higher ground soon. A large snake draped on a rotting tree limb sprang in an attack at the intruders passing through his home. Luckily for Delilah and Marcus, the snake narrowly missed its target and recoiled back onto itself, ready for its next unfortunate victim. Perhaps they would not be as lucky as these two.

They had to stop and get their bearings as they had not spotted any pearls in a while and were no longer sure of the direction. Delilah called out for help, hoping someone anyone would hear them and come to their aid, but all they heard were those incessant insect sounds.

They continued in a northeasterly direction, sure that it was the way to safety as the ground was getting drier and firmer. Marcus was growing weary but would not stop. This man had saved him twice, he was not about to fail him now. Suddenly, there in the dirt shimmered another pearl; at least they were going in the right direction.

Jameson began to wheeze and cough as blood came out of his mouth and nostrils. This was not a good sign and Delilah was in a panic, though she kept telling Jameson he would be alright and they would be together again soon, safe at Serenity.

A noise broke through the relentless droning; it was Jebediah and the men from Serenity carrying torches. They were coming to search for Jameson and Delilah. She called out to them and in a manner of seconds they were found.

"Aunt Delilah, oh my God, what happened here?"

"James was stabbed by that Frenchman."

"Where is he, I'll kill him."

"He's already dead; we need to get James to a doctor, now."

Jebediah yelled out, "One of you men go to town and bring back the doctor now. Tell him it is an emergency, Jameson's been hurt bad, hurry."

Together, Marcus and Jebediah carried the weakened body of Jameson and followed the trail of men that would lead out of the swamp.

Delilah kept talking to Jameson, telling him how much she loved him and to keep fighting for his life, but the blood discharging from the wound was not a good sign and they needed to hurry. Every minute counted, it was a matter of life and death.

# Chapter 23

# *No Time to Lose*

The small band of heroes were running as fast as they could, dodging low hanging tree branches, rocks and rotting limbs that peppered the ground. Jameson's tourniquet that Delilah had diligently applied was filled with blood and trickling onto the ground, it had not stopped the bleeding. He was still coughing up blood.

The clearing lie ahead and soon they were back onto the plantation. The two men carried Jameson into the house and laid him on the sofa in the den. Nanny told them to boil water and get her sewing kit; she would cleanse the wound and stitch him up hoping the bleeding would stop. Luckily Nanny was not severely hurt by Michelle, just a sprain to her back.

Everyone cooperated and performed their assigned task without hesitation. Jameson was pale and Delilah kept talking to him to keep his spirits up.

"I love you, James. Just wait until you are better, we will be going back to Boston and we will have a new child. Life will be great for us, just you hold on."

Nanny unwrapped the bandage and was shocked at the amount of blood pouring out of the wound. Jameson was pale and cold, that was not a good sign. She attempted to wash the area as Jameson winced in pain.

"Nanny, hurry up and stitch the wound. He's lost a lot of blood."

"I'm trying honey, I'm trying."

She threaded the needle and pierced his skin pulling the thread through and into the next hole. She completed her task and pulled the threads tightly to close the wound. Within seconds blood pooled under the wound, it was clear the sword had pierced a major blood vessel and would not be stopped. Jameson was bleeding to death and they needed the doctor to help him. Someone would have to go inside and stitch up the blood vessel, Nanny could not do that. She applied pressure, hoping the blood would clot and stop the flow. Jameson started to cough and was spitting up blood. Nanny was afraid she was forcing the blood into another direction and reopened the wound.

Jameson whispered, "Delilah, I love you. I always will love you. Hold me tight."

"Mommy is daddy alright? Why does he look so sick?" inquired little Dawnalee.

Delilah yelled at the children, "Go outside and stay there. Everything is going to be alright." She did not want them to see their father in this condition.

Everyone was pacing back and forth and praying for the doctor to arrive. It seemed like hours had passed but only precious minutes ticked away.

Delilah grew more concerned and continued to speak to her husband in the hopes of keeping his spirits up, "James, you are the most wonderful man in the world. I am so happy to have met you and to be your wife. I want to grow old with you. Do you hear me? I don't want to live without you."

Tears were in her eyes as she held Jameson in her arms. He was growing weaker and all color had left his face. They tried to give him some water to drink but he could not swallow anything.

"You get better, do you hear me," she cried, "I have a whole life to live with you yet. You haven't met your new child yet. James, James, don't leave me."

Doctor Robert Pritchard finally arrived and raced over to his patient. He looked at the wound, felt for a pulse, listened to his heart and chest and then looked at Delilah. The expression on his face told the whole story.

"I'm so sorry, Delilah, I am too late. The wound has punctured a major artery and he has lost too much blood, there is nothing I can do. I'm sorry."

"No, no that can't be possible," Delilah cried.

She bent over to kiss Jameson as his body went limp and the last breath left his body. He lie motionless in her arms, as a warm breeze blew over him and out into the night sky. She was silent for a second. She could not believe what had happened. Then she screamed in agony, burst into tears and fell onto his lifeless body.

"No, no this can't be happening. I love you James, you can't be gone. I won't let you go. You come back to me, you hear me, my love, and you come back to me, right now. Oh God, please don't take this man from me. I love him so much. Please let him live."

Nanny knelt down next to her and put her arms around them both and broke into tears. She loved him like a son and her heart was breaking also.

Madeline, Jebediah, Marcus and Ambrosia all knelt down and placed their arms around each other, crying and weeping for their dear friend.

Delilah would not be consoled and kept crying and crying. Dawnalee and Ruby Rose had returned inside the house hearing the cries from Delilah. They did not fully understand what had happened, but the sight of their mother being so sad and forlorn made them cry right along with mommy. Delilah had to be coaxed off of Jameson's body and once free she ran back again hoping the outcome would be different and he would breathe again and his eyes would open and he would look at her and smile that smile that she so loved, but she would never see it again, except in her memory. She was heartbroken that she would never be with him, hold him in her arms, kiss his lips, or feel his presence in her life. She was alone again and desperately wanted him back, if only for a brief second, just to be able to tell him, she loved him, but that was not to be.

Delilah and Nanny cried through the night and into the morning. Dawnalee asked where her father was and Delilah tried to explain to her and her sister that he had gone away to a better place, to be with God. Dawnalee wanted to know why he had not taken them with him, she wanted her daddy back.

"Tell God to bring him back, mommy, I want my daddy back."

Delilah held both of them and tried to provide comfort but they both felt the emptiness and wept for the loss of the greatest man they had ever known.

Jameson Hartford, the man who fought for equality, freedom and justice was gone, but he would never be forgotten, as long as his story would continue to be told from one person to another, generation unto generation.

# Chapter 24

## *Eulogy*

The whole town turned out for the funeral of their friend, Jameson Hartford and everyone expressed their deepest sympathy to the grieving widow. All were dressed in black to mourn their friend. His life had touched many other lives and had brought equality and happiness to many people.

Abigail had survived and so had her child. Anabelle had also survived but had a broken jaw and was severely bruised and scarred. She would never be the beauty she was before, that gift had been taken from her, perhaps because she abused it and used it for evil instead of good. She remained in the shadows, not wanting anyone to see her disfigurement and her shame. She wept all by herself watching from afar.

As they gathered at the wake, Nanny was the first to speak.

"Mista Jameson was a great man. He always treated me with respect, even when others didn't. He stood up for what was right and just when others didn't care. I know he wasn't, but I always felt like he was my son and he always treated me like I was his mother. I will think about him every day and will miss him so much."

She raised her eyes to heaven and said," I know you're looking down on us, Mista Jameson but you have no idea how much we all miss you down here. I'll be looking forward to the time when I can be with you again."

Nanny broke down in tears and had to be escorted back to her seat. Many others paid tribute to the great man, including Jebediah, Madeline, Ambrosia, Marcus, Azure, Sienna and Doctor Pritchard, but when Abigail got up, no one knew what to expect.

She looked at Delilah and asked, "May I please say a few words, Delilah?"

Delilah shook her head yes. Abigail approached the lectern.

"I knew Jameson for many years. You all know that I was his first wife, but what you may not know is that I never stopped loving him. He was a truly great man, who stood up for what he believed in and tried to convince others to see things his way. I should have, but I was too blind to see that he was right and I was wrong. I lost him to another and always regretted it. I should have been there when he needed me and I was not. I regret my actions every day and I will until the day I die. He found another and he and Delilah were perfect for each other. They made each other happy which is what you are supposed to do when you are husband and wife, something I could never do. I love you Jameson and always will and I will miss you every day of my life; and if Delilah will let me, I would like to be friends with her and be sure that both our children know what a wonderful man their father was, so we and they never forget him, ever."

Abigail went over to Delilah, hugged her and asked for forgiveness and friendship.

The last to speak was Delilah, fighting back the tears with all her strength.

"My husband was the greatest man I have ever known. He saved me from a life of slavery and gave me a whole new life filled with love and a child. But it did not come easy; he lost everything in the process, his friends, his family, his plantation, his job, everything, but he never wavered in his conviction that all men were created equal, regardless of race, creed or color. He took a poor slave girl and made her his equal and his wife. He didn't care about the consequences and he suffered for his beliefs, trust me. As I stand here today and look out at this gathering of all our friends and relatives, I see his dream come to fruition. You are all standing together, side by side as one group of God's people. He would be happy and proud. It is what he wanted all along."

Stopping to wipe the tears and compose herself, she continued, "James, I will miss you more than you will ever know. You were my love, my strength and my life; my friend and companion as we went through life. I did not get to have you long enough, but at least I got to have you, for even a lifetime would not be long enough. I will dream about you every night and will hear your voice in my ears forever. I will never forget you, my love and only hope that one day I may be worthy enough to see you again in heaven, because if any man is there, you are there my sweetheart looking down on all of us and smiling."

Delilah started crying uncontrollably and fell to her knees. Madeline rushed to her aid and helped her back to her feet. A fresh handkerchief was forthcoming and tears were once again dried from her face. She began to make her way back to her seat, then turned around to add one more thing.

"James once told me an adage that was related to him by a traveling salesman. He believed it was a Cherokee Indian saying. It went: *"When you were born, you cried and the world rejoiced; live your life so that when you die, the world cries and you rejoice."* Looking out on all of you today,

I believe he succeeded. Thank you all for coming, James and I appreciate it very much."

Delilah began to cry once again and fell over the coffin sobbing, "James, James, why did you leave me. I want you back here with me so bad, I love you my darling."

Nanny and Madeline had to help her back to her seat. She held tightly onto little Dawnalee and her sister Ruby Red, her only connections to the man she loved so dearly. One by one all the mourners filed by the wooden coffin and placed a flower upon it. Most left a tear along with the blossom.

The black mourners began to sing a spiritual they had learned while toiling in the fields asking Jesus to give them strength and save them. The white mourners quickly learned the melody and joined in. United in song and sorrow, they praised the Lord and the man who had finally brought them together. Then they broke into a familiar chorus; tears flowed as their voices joined together as one:

*Glory, glory hallelujah, glory, glory hallelujah, glory, glory hallelujah, his truth is marching on.*

Jameson Lee Hartford was laid to rest at Serenity in the family grave yard. A huge granite stone marked the location.

Delilah, Dawnalee, Ruby Rose and Nanny placed fresh flowers on it every day for the rest of their lives. Many of the townspeople regularly visited the gravesite and prayed for the man and thanked God for being blessed to have known him. His final resting place was always filled with flowers and thankful messages from a grateful community.

# Chapter 25

## *Epilogue*

In the next few days, Jebediah and Marcus, in an attempt to give some hope to a grieving Delilah, returned to the swamp with an idea. They wanted to find and recover Delilah's pearls, restring them and surprise her with a new strand. They knew this small gesture would make her happy and perhaps they could bring a smile to her face once again, a smile that no one had seen since the tragic death of her beloved husband. It would be difficult, they imagined, as the mud and soft earth would cover and disguise the jewels, preventing the light from revealing their whereabouts. They also had to watch out for the reptiles, quicksand and poison plants that thrived in this inhospitable habitat.

They searched carefully marking their steps so as not to get lost in the forbidden area. There was one and look there, another. They still glistened even in the minimal amount of sunlight that was allowed to pierce through the dense overgrowth. They walked all the way back to the clearing and the old shack, amassing quite a few gems. When they were satisfied that they had found as many as was possible, they returned home. They even managed to find the original string that Delilah had torn off her neck.

They imagined it was a sign and maybe Jameson was guiding them, at least that was the way they felt.

They returned them to Madeline and Ambrosia who carefully cleaned each one, and painstakingly began to restring them. Marcus was even able to repair the broken clasp. When it was completed, the necklace almost looked as good as new, no one would be able to tell the difference.

That afternoon they surprised Delilah with a box. They had to coax her to open it as she was distraught and not in the mood for a present or cheering up of any kind. Upon opening the box and seeing the pearls glowing in the light, she was touched by their generosity and kindness and wept with joy. She hugged and kissed each one in turn and then she placed it around her neck and clasped it tight; where it was never to be removed again. She immediately felt closer to James and Martha and it gave her a feeling of inner peace.

Six months later, Delilah delivered a healthy baby boy which she promptly named, Jameson Lee Hartford Jr. He was the spitting image of his father.

Abigail too delivered a child, a girl which she named, Jamie Gail, a tribute to her former husband. She had a difficult pregnancy and a very hard delivery due to the wound she suffered at the hands of the Frenchman.

Delilah and she became unlikely friends but complications continued to plague Abigail, the wound would not permanently heal and she never fully recuperated. One day Delilah's presence was requested at Tall Oaks. When she entered Abigail's room, she was aghast at how pale and weak the lady had become. Doctor Pritchard told her Abigail was near death how and there was nothing more he could do. Her spirit seemed unwilling or unable to go on.

Abigail summoned Delilah close to her bed and managed to acquire the strength to speak, "Delilah, I'm not going to make it."

"Don't talk like that; of course you will Abbey, you're going to get better."

"No, no I know I won't, but I need to ask you a big favor."

"Of course, Abigail, you can ask me anything, but there is no need as you will get better, just as before."

"I need you to take care of Jamie Gail for me. I know that is a lot to ask, but you're the only one I trust to raise her."

"What about Annabelle?"

"Belle, she's still such a scatterbrain can't possibly raise a baby. She is still not well since the, er…incident. Please do this for me…and Jameson…please."

Delilah did not have to think twice about the request, after all, the baby was a part of Jameson and she knew he would want her to take care of his child.

"Of course I will, Abigail, I will raise her as if she was my own child, don't you worry about that; but you rest and try to get better so you can…"

Suddenly Abigail went silent and quietly passed. It seemed as if she held onto life just long enough to secure her daughters future. Doc Pritchard felt her pulse, listened to her heart and sadly covered her with a sheet.

Delilah and Annabelle cried together, all hate and jealousy had been forgotten. Delilah took the child home with her that day and lived up to her promise.

Annabelle was ridden with guilt because of what she had started with the Frenchman. She blamed herself for Jameson's death, her sister's death and for her own disfigurement. She was severely depressed. Once her sister passed, she had no reason to continue and it only took a few short months before she died of remorse and loneliness.

Delilah together with Nanny would raise the children. They would tell them bedtime stories about their father and what a great man he was, making him seem larger than life to the impressionable young minds, all the while instilling in them the principles of fairness, equality and love. The children adored the stories and always asked for another, while always being mindful of their mother and listening to her every word.

Nanny survived for 5 more years and then one night passed peacefully in her sleep. She was buried next to her dear friend and secret love, Uncky. All mourned the loss of this great lady, friend and adopted mother. They were all blessed to have known such a wonderful human being and would forever feel her loss. She was the voice of reason so many times and helped them through all their trials and blessings. No one could ever replace her and she would never be forgotten.

Jebediah and Madeline had two children of their own and stayed on to run the plantation and care for the heartbroken Delilah and her three children.

Dawnalee, Jameson Jr., Ruby Rose and Jamie Gail all went to university after high school, Delilah insisted on a good education. They graduated with honors and decided on their life's work. Ruby Rose grew up to be a teacher ensuring all her pupils would have a good education and racism would be a thing of the past. Jameson Jr. grew up to be a lawyer specializing in cases for the poor and downtrodden. He had a lot of his father in him. Jamie Gail grew up to be an activist, crusading for equality and minority rights. Dawnalee had a penchant for numbers and eventually returned to Boston, settled there and ran the bank her father had started. They all married and had children of their own, thus insuring the lineage of the Hartford name and its crusade for righteousness and equality.

Delilah never left Serenity. She wanted to remain close to where her dear departed husband was buried. She worked part time, but mostly spent her days taking care of the children. She learned a valuable lesson, that money meant nothing without love. She blamed herself for not spending more time with Jameson while he was alive instead of pursuing her business interests which seemed so unimportant now. She never remarried as she said no man could ever replace her first love and soul mate, Jameson. She kept her hair short for Jameson and would spend every evening, after dinner, sitting on the front porch, smoking a cigar and talking to him. No one knew for sure if his soul was indeed there or not; but a warm wind seemed to well out of nowhere and softly caress her, assuring Delilah her James was near.

Delilah lived to the ripe old age of 89 and when she died, she was surrounded by her children and grandchildren and all her friends and family. One night, as she laid in her bed a warm breeze wafted through the room and then slowly out the window leaving Delilah with a huge smile on her face. It was as if Jameson had come to touch her and take her with him to their eternal reward.

She was buried next to her beloved Jameson. The large stone marker is still there today and the engraving is still visible. It reads:

*Jameson and Delilah Hartford – Together again…forever*

And so they still are and will always be.